# STEEPED IN
# TEA

## creative ideas, activities & recipes for tea lovers

STOREY
BOOKS

*The mission of Storey Communications is to serve our customers by publishing practical information that encourages personal independence in harmony with the environment.*

Edited by Deborah Balmuth and Robin Catalano

Cover design and interior concept by Carol Jessop, Black Trout Design

Interior design, photo styling, layout, and graphics by Jen Rork

Illustrations by Kathy Bray

Photographs on pages 3, 4, 11, 24, 25, 31, 41, 49, 60, 61, 77, 79, 87, 95, 103, 105, 106, 114, 115 by John Conte; pages 147 and 151 by Jerry Pavia; page 145 by Sarut, NYC; all others by Giles Prett.

Indexed by Indexes & Knowledge Maps

Bristish and Contemporary tea caddies pictured on page 28 courtesy of Library Antiques, Williamstown, MA.

Storey books are available for special premium and promotional uses and for customized editions. For further information, please call Storey's Custom Publishing Department at 1-800-793-9396.

The information in this book is true and complete to the best of our knowledge. All recommendations are made without guarantee on the part of the author or Storey Books. The author and publisher disclaim any liability in connection with the use of this information. For additional information please contact Storey Books, Schoolhouse Road, Pownal, Vermont 05261.

Printed in Canada by Transcontinental Printing
10 9 8 7 6 5 4 3 2 1

**Library of Congress Cataloging-in-Publication Data**

Rosen, Diana
    Steeped in tea : creative ideas, activities & recipes for tea lovers / Diana Rosen
       p.  cm.
    Includes bibliographical references and index.
    ISBN 1-58017-093-5 (pbk. : alk. paper)
    1. Title.  2. Tea—History.  3. Afternoon teas.  4. Cookery.
  I. Title.
TX415.R684   1999
641.3'372—dc21                    98-47384
                                            CIP

# contents

## dedication

To the memory of Mrs. Elizabeth Reagan (1881–1975),
the Martha Stewart of Delaware Avenue.

## acknowledgments

Thank-you to Chef Robert Wemischner for his creative recipes for cooking with tea; to Gary Stotsky, Amy Ulmer, Marge Glantz, and the late Esther Maxwell for additional recipes; to Diane Tortolano, Dona Schweiger, Sally Champe, Patti Anastasi, and Carolyn Manzi for innovative ideas using tea in crafts and home accessories; and to editors Deborah Balmuth and Robin Catalano of Storey Books for enthusiasm, judicious blue penciling, and unwavering support.

# an invitation

C ome for tea.

Have you had your tea today?

Let's put the kettle on and we'll all have tea.

Tea, steeped to perfection, offers a taste and fragrance that says *welcome* — wherever you live or travel. Hospitality is that warm gesture to strangers and friends alike from a sympathetic person who says, "Come in, make yourself at home, my house is your house." They are two separate words, but, for most of the world's population, *tea* and *hospitality* are one and the same thing.

## TEA AROUND THE WORLD

Visit a home in India and in the back corner of the main room you'll see a tea table at the ready. Teapot, teacups, creamer and sugar bowl, and tea cozy are always available to serve guests — expected or not.

Step into a Moroccan shop or home and you're sure to see the *sitya,* the classic, three-legged brass tray. On this tray sits the traditional teapot with a long, thin, graceful spout used to pour fresh mint green tea into little glasses for your refreshment. To the Moroccan, offering tea is like saying, "Hello, happy to see you. I thank you for coming to see me."

### Eastern Traditions

Tea is drunk all day long in China, the birthplace of this famous brew, where everyone drinks tea just as naturally as they

*The sitya, or three-legged brass tray, is a standard item in most Moroccon homes.*

breathe. Should you pass a friend on the street, you might be asked, "Do you have leisure time today? Time to have tea?" And of course everyone has time for tea; the delicate green tea that is the nation's everyday tea, or the intentionally aged pu-erh, a digestive tea that is calming and healthful to drink all day and all night long. In the fields, in the cities, on the bays, everyone offers tea at the same time they say hello.

You can enjoy tea in many different ceremonies and drinking styles, from the refined to the casual. Consider *gung fu,* miniature cups and tiny pots, an elegant presentation commonly used to serve tea in Taiwan and so perfectly matched to the intense, mouth-caressing flavor

*The gung-fu set, used to serve tea in Taiwan, is a popular tea collectible.*

of that country's signature tea, oolong. The delicacy of the preparation and the attention to detail demonstrate once again a form of welcome — a graceful hospitality. It is not incidental that *gung fu* translates to "the art and skill of doing things well."

Visiting Japan, you will be served "guest tea," a green tea that is palate cleansing and refreshing. Although the elaborate and formal tea ceremony of *chanoyu* is an integral part of Japan's culture, it is not an everyday experience. Instead, as in China, tea is drunk all day long from breakfast on. Japanese tea is either a softly astringent or a roasted green that is pleasant for everyone, from children to seniors.

## Western Traditions

In England, everything stops for tea: elevenses in the morning with a cup of tea and a biscuit at the office or at home; four o'clock for dessert or scones and tea, or a more elaborate dainty menu of scones, sandwiches, sweets, and tea. In the north country, tea is at six o'clock; it's a light meal. When you visit any part of Great Britain, the first words you'll hear after hello are, "I'll put the kettle on."

*While expensive tea caddies used to be the favored place for tea storage, the average kitchen canister is ideal.*

In 17th-century France, Dr. Gui Patin, already famous for being an enemy of innovation, referred to tea as "this impertinent novelty of the century." Despite his protests, and those of other prominent physicians of the time, tea has had a long and treasured existence in France, particularly in Paris society.

The most eloquent of 17th-century letter writers, Madame de Sévigné (Marie de Rabutin-chantal, Marquise de Sévigné), often remarked on the health benefits of tea drinking and tea service among her many aristocratic friends. She attributes to her friend Madame de la Sablière the first occasion of putting milk into tea. In one of her charming letters, she comments that the princess of Tarente took 12 cups of tea daily and Monsieur le Landgrave 40. "He was dying," she wrote, "and this [tea] resuscitated him visibly."

While London had its elaborate afternoon hour devoted to the pleasure of tea, Paris was creating its own tradition. The Parisian five o'clock began rather modestly in a stationer's shop owned by the Neal brothers on rue de Rivoli in 1900. Anxious to please customers fatigued from the awesome decisions of selecting personal stationery, the brothers started serving biscuits and tea on two small tables at the end of their sales counter.

This modest effort to refresh customers and keep them in the store longer had far-reaching effects throughout Paris, garnering imitators in department stores, bistros, and tearooms — which sprung up all over Paris. Today, you can cement friendships or do business over marvelous pastries served with exceptionally fine teas at any number of *salons du thé,* or tea salons.

## THE HISTORY OF TEA

True tea comes from the *Camellia sinensis* bush, which is now grown in 35 countries around the world (and in very modest amounts in the United States by American Classic Tea). First discovered by the Chinese emperor S'heng Nung in 2737 B.C., tea was soon introduced to India, Japan, and other pan-Asian countries, primarily by monks who drank this beverage as a way to keep alert during their long meditations.

Today's scientists have confirmed what a billion Chinese and their ancestors have known for nearly five thousand years: Tea is good for you. It's healthful to drink and beneficial to use topically; its powerful antioxidants, called polyphenols, are important in fighting disease.

Tea's incredible variety of taste characteristics reflects the style and intensity of processing, which result in the definitive tea types: white, yellow, green, oolong, black, and pu-erh. The leaves, all from the same plant, *Camellia sinensis,* can be transformed into any one of these types by careful processing via air drying, pan firing in woks, machine heating, or light steaming. Then, depending on the individual processor in each region of each country, the tea leaves can be hand or machine rolled and processed further to create a taste unique to that area. This nearly endless choice is what makes tea so fascinating and so popular: It is the most-consumed beverage in the world, after water.

## Beginnings

Tea is such a strong presence in billions of people's daily lives that it is hard to imagine that in its early history tea was strictly the province of royalty, the priesthood, and the well-to-do. In its beginnings, tea even separated classes instead of bringing them together.

When first exported to England in the 17th century, tea was so novel and so expensive that tea caddies were built with lock and key so that the mistress of the house could keep her precious bohea and hyson (black and green teas) hidden from servants.

## Tea in the Modern Age

During the 19th and 20th centuries, thanks to modern machinery and production methods and expert distribution systems, tea became

## teas mentioned in this book

The teas mentioned in the chart on pages 6–7 are only a few of the thousands of teas one can enjoy, each intriguing in its own way. When using high-quality teas, it is better to use slightly cooler temperatures for slightly less brewing time, which enables you to have at least two and sometimes four or more infusions from the original amount of tea. As always, let your own palate be the ultimate guide. If you like stronger tea infuse longer, but always decant the tea; if you allow the leaves to stay in the water, the tea will turn bitter. For excess tea liquor, pour into a second smaller teapot or a creamer and pour refills from that.

Unless otherwise noted, all of these teas should be drunk plain. Some recipes are for 6 ounces and some are for 4 ounces of water; the smaller amounts are for the more delicate teas, which should be infused more than once, rather than making one larger serving that will diffuse the flavor.

# a guide to teas

| Origin | Name | Description |
|---|---|---|
| Africa | Kenya | A clear, clean, crisp black tea terrific with sweets or a hearty meal. Very refreshing and palate cleansing. |
| China | Keemun | A black tea of beautiful red liquor and sweetish finish; hearty and satisfying alone and a distinctive addition to blends. |
| China | Lapsang Souchong | A strong, smoky tea that is dried over wood. Can be drunk with lemon or plain. |
| China | Pu-erh | An intentionally aged black tea, pu-erh is an excellent digestive following heavy meals. |
| China | Yunnan | Available either as black or green with a natural sweet finish. Goes particularly well with a meal. |
| India | Darjeeling | The champagne of teas, elegant in the dried state and fragrant in the cup. Also available in green and oolong. |
| India | Masala Chai | A tea drink usually made with poor-grade black tea and exotic spices. The better the tea used, the better the chai. |
| India | Nilgiri Black | Nilgiri is terrific iced or hot because it is naturally fruity; doesn't cloud when iced. |
| Sri Lanka | Ceylon Black | Crisp, clean, refreshing, excellent with foods. Adds a brightness to blends. |
| Generic | Sun Tea | For best flavor use a Nilgiri or Ceylon. |

| Origin | Name | Description |
|---|---|---|
| Blend | Earl Grey | A blend of China or Indian blacks and oil of bergamot, a Mediterranean, pear-shaped citrus fruit. |
| Blend | English Breakfast | A combination of Keemun for fragrance, Ceylon for brightness, and Assam for heartiness. |
| Blend | Irish Breakfast | Same as above, but usually a heartier blend, with more emphasis on Assam. |
| Blend | Russian Caravan | Named for caravans of camels that trekked the Silk Road route from China to Russia. It has a smoky tang and aroma. |

| Origin | Name | Description |
|---|---|---|
| China | Shou Mei | A white tea shaped into small curved "eyebrows" that unfurl gracefully when brewed. |
| China | Silver Needle | Elegant with long leaves, this actually is a delicate white, best served in a tumbler. |
| China & Taiwan | Ti Kwan Yin | An oolong tea of exquisite fragrance and full-mouth taste that quite often defies words. |
| Japan | Genmaicha | A mild nutty-tasting green tea mixed with roasted rice and, yes, it really does have popcorn in it. |
| Japan | Gyokuro | The "precious dew" of green teas, this is the most costly Japanese tea. |
| Japan | Sencha | Excellent green tea, lightly steamed and refreshing, perfect as a "guest tea" or with meals. |

Brew 1 teaspoon of leaves with 6 ounces of 200°F spring
water for about 2 minutes, or more to taste.

Brew a rounded teaspoon in 6 ounces of 195–200°F
spring water for 2–3 minutes.

Brew 1 heaping teaspoon in 6 ounces of 200°F spring water
for 2–3 minutes

Brew 1 teaspoon in 6 ounces of roiling boiling spring water
for 2–3 minutes, or longer to taste.

Brew 1 teaspoon in 6 ounces of 195–200°F spring water for
about 2–3 minutes for black and 2 minutes or less for green.

Brew 1 level teaspoon for about two minutes in 6 ounces of spring
water heated to about 195°F; brew longer if you want a stronger taste.

Brew the tea and the spices for at least 15–20 minutes; add
milk and heat again; strain and serve.

Brew 1 heaping teaspoon in 6 ounces of 195–200°F spring
water for about 2 minutes, or more to taste.

Brew 1 rounded teaspoon in 6 ounces spring water heated
to just under boiling, about 195–200°F, for 3 minutes.

In the morning, set out a clear gallon jar with either 10 teabags or 10 heaping
teaspoons tea leaves. At lunchtime, strain, add ice, and savor.

Brew 1 teaspoon tea in 6 ounces of 195–200°F spring water
for about 2 minutes.

Brew 1 heaping teaspoon in nearly boiling (about 200°F)
spring water for about 2 minutes. Excellent with milk.

Brew as above. Also tastes good with milk.

Brew 1 heaping teaspoon in 6 ounces of 200°F spring
water for about 3 minutes, or more to taste.

Brew 1 teaspoon leaves in 6 ounces of 175–185°F spring
water for 1 minute; taste. Best to reinfuse with subsequent cups.

Brew about 1 heaping teaspoon in 4 ounces of 175–185°F spring
water for 1 minute. Subsequent cups take on more flavor.

Brew 1 level teaspoon in 4 ounces of 185–195°F spring water
for about 2 minutes. Can be reinfused several times.

To brew, use 1 heaping teaspoon in 6 ounces of nearly boiling
(about 200°F) spring water for about 3 minutes.

Brew about 1 level teaspoon of the vivid hunter green leaves in about 4 ounces
of 185–190°F spring water for about 2 minutes. Can be reinfused several times.

Brew 1 teaspoon of tea in 6 ounces of 185–190°F spring
water for about 2 minutes.

more moderately priced and more readily available to "the masses." As we approach the 21st century, tea has found renewed popularity — to the point that some teas have developed a certain connoisseur cachet. These teas are beautiful to look at and exotic to taste; they can cost hundreds to thousands of dollars per pound.

Parallel to the rise in tea's popularity has been a growth in the number of places to enjoy tea: the intensely social tea gardens of 17th- and 18th-century England; the quiet, ritualized teahouses of Japan; the tearooms throughout the southern United States, where white gloves and hats set a tone of gentility; and many others.

As enjoyable as it is to savor tea in public teahouses or tea salons, the experience is even more pleasant in the comfort and privacy of your home. Toward that end, I have created this book to give you ideas for tea experiences and projects using tea for every room in the house, along with the garden. Among the ideas are serene tea havens for your solo enjoyment and exceptional party formats for elaborate or intimate gatherings where tea can be the conduit for relaxing with friends, nurturing your family relationships, or softening the business meeting or volunteer activity.

## TEA FOR EVERY PART OF YOUR LIFE

Tea is an international beverage, yet you needn't travel thousands of miles to enjoy it at a dacha or on a croquet lawn. Fine teaware is a readily available pleasure, and you don't need to invest a fortune to collect pieces. Tea themes can be a vivid part of your personal accessories, the gifts you create, and your office or home decor.

Tea can also be a part of your personal beauty regime or an innovative ingredient in everyday cooking. Its versatility means even leftover tea and spent tea leaves are useful in home and garden projects.

Come, let me show you how to create a life steeped in tea, in every room of the home and in the garden.

# part one
## CREATING AN ATMOSPHERE FOR TEA

no one on his or her deathbed ever said, "I wish I'd dusted more . . . I wish I'd spent more time at work . . . I wish I'd watched more television." More likely, we'll hear regrets of not loving more, not spending more time with friends and family, not enjoying more of life's simpler pleasures . . . like savoring a cup of tea.

Four words that should be struck from our vocabulary are *I don't have time.* If you truly enjoy something, there is always time. We *all* have *all* the time we need to do *all* that we have to do. It is up to us, every day, to prioritize our "things to do" list to include those essentials that we know give us happiness and make our lives worth living. In fact, many studies have shown that doing something you enjoy every day extends your life and makes you happier and more productive.

Why, then, do we sometimes feel that taking a few minutes to drink a cup of tea is an indulgence? Are you concerned that others may believe taking time out for tea is a trivial act? The answer is to turn the tables on those outside critics and invite them to join you. They'll quickly realize that this respite not only allows for pleasant companionship, but it also provides the benefit of the regenerative qualities of tea. What if the critic is actually you? Tell that overly serious inner voice to lighten up, sip a cup, and be good to you.

Still think you shouldn't "waste time" on tea? Please be informed that as head of Tea Enthusiasts Anonymous (T.E.A.), I am here to tell you that tea is not only a good use of your time, but it is an absolute essential to the civilized life. By *civilized* I don't mean pinky-in-the-air civilized; I mean a life so satisfying that its pleasures soothe and uplift, not unlike the tea itself.

Creating an atmosphere for tea is more than designing a comfortable backdrop for drinking our favorite brew. It's living consciously, deeply, and richly; it's sharing with others. Drinking tea is like meditation, giving us a sense of peace, drawing us closer to our friends and family, taking us to our deepest thoughts and feelings, bringing us to that core, that sense of being home. Serenity is the greatest benefit of a life with tea, and it takes so little to achieve it.

What can you do to design a permanent place for drinking tea wherever and whenever you want? Take the time right now to walk around your home, be it a one-room studio, a three-room flat, or a multiroom manse. What can you add or take away so that each room says *welcome?*

*Take time for a delightful experience by creating an atmosphere for tea.*

Making each room in your house and place in your garden attractive is something all of us understand. Being able to look around your living room at photos of people you adore is like feeling their embraces even when they're not actually in the room. Using the good silver or best china whenever you feel like it is a gift of pleasure you give to yourself and others. Touching, looking at, and using your treasures are the reasons you have them in the first place. While finding just the right materials to build the nest, the cave, the house, or other shelter that will be protection from the elements is important, there is much more to it. Shelter is just protection; it is only when you live with love, gratitude, and peace that a nest truly becomes "home."

Throughout this book are suggestions both major and quite minor to help you live with a more decided grace, a deeper commitment to making today valuable. When you adopt the habit of the tea life, today becomes the day you stop to listen to a child, read a poem, tell people what you like or admire about them, create something with your hands, plant a flower, or otherwise spend your time well.

Creating an atmosphere in your home, business, or garden that is dedicated solely to the pleasures of tea is the ultimate act of kindness to yourself and to others. Taking time for tea is a metaphor for taking time for you. For our tour of the home and garden steeped in tea, let's begin in those public and social rooms that lend themselves so easily to the camaraderie of tea pleasures.

# tea in the living room

Soft golds and grays, French Provincial cherrywood furniture, downy chairs and sofas. These were the elements of the gracious living room of my family home. It was truly a living room, for company, for play, for quiet or boisterous times.

The upholstered furnishings had those elegant braided fringes, wonderful to knot or tie dolls to; they also served as mini curtains from which my sister and I would peek out to see if the other had figured out our secret hiding places. Over and over again, we reenacted the famous scene in *Singin' in the Rain* when Debbie Reynolds, Donald O'Connor, and Gene Kelly danced up and over and upside down on the sofa. We ate popcorn while watching our elderly sleeping babysitter do her amazing mouth-cheek-nose snore, more entertainment than *Sky King* on a Saturday morning.

The living room was a theater, where my parents could "attend" Broadway plays that had been recorded, or dance to Big Band tunes, or sit quietly listening to tranquil chamber music while my father read and my mother knitted.

Visiting family held court: Our aunts told stories about their brother or sister — my parents — convincing my sister and me that, yes, our parents were once children, too. Cousins taught us new dance steps, silly riddles and jokes, and even when it was just the immediate four of us the living room was where we made our own memorable (and free!) entertainment.

That living room is more often than not an anachronism these days. Many families spend much of their time in casual, TV-centered family rooms or, more often, separated by activities elsewhere. The living room is too often relegated to company-only events instead of company-best behavior directed toward each other.

Creating a living room "tea spot" can change how you use the room. With furnishings geared toward casual comfort over style, convenience over stringent interior design, the tea-infused living room helps everyone relax and have a good time. Here you can play board, card, or word games, or make a space in which to watch the plays children create. Perhaps you'd rather hold family concerts with live music, or enjoy a well-stocked CD library.

What about that 20th-century marvel, television? It certainly can stimulate conversation, but turn it off and conversation gains another dimension: It becomes more amusing, more informative, and as dramatic as anything ever broadcast.

Tea is as easily shared among family as with friends, and the only "ambience" required is an effort to demonstrate that you care, you want to share the warmth of a cup of tea and the nourishment of a small snack, and, most important, you want to give family and friends your most precious gift: time.

## FAMILY TEA

A family tea behind your newly crafted screen (for project see page 16) can be anything enjoyed by the entire family, from popcorn to popovers.

What follows is a light-spirited menu for all ages:

- Genmaicha tea
- Crudités of baby vegetables (e.g., fennel, radishes, carrots, or other favorites)
- Dill Dip
- Hors d'ouevres
- Chocolates

Savor the treats and one another!

now stir the fire, and close the shutters fast,
Let fall the curtain, wheel the sofa round,
And while the bubbling and loud hissing urn
Throws up a steamy column; and the cups
That cheer but not inebriate, wait on each,
So let us welcome peaceful evening in.

— WILLIAM COWPER,
"The Task" (1785)

## VICTORIAN FOLDING SCREEN

**LEVEL OF EXPERTISE:**
easy

**TOOLS AND MATERIALS:**
ruler or tape measure

commercial folding screen

large Kraft or butcher
     paper for layouts

pencil

decoupage items

regular scissors

manicure scissors

rubber cement

clear varnish (polyurethane
     is excellent)

brush for varnish

This idea is actually a throwback to a craft many women practiced during the Victorian era as a way to show off Valentine's Day cards or treasured paper ephemera: decoupage on folding screens. This simple technique of cutting out paper images, gluing them onto an object, and preserving them with a clear finish is easy, fun, and useful. I have kept many cards, letters, gift tags and wraps, sachet envelopes, photographs, and souvenir menus featuring teapots and teacups because they're simply too delightful to throw away. Creating a decorative folding screen seemed an ideal way to give a second life to all the beautiful tea-themed items that, over the years, had caught my eye.

The Victorian Folding Screen is something the entire family can put together in an evening or over a casual weekend. Pre-made folding screens are inexpensive and readily available, or you can try making your own. Because it is so easy to move around, the folding screen will be useful to set off a tea-drinking section in any room of your home. It will be a constant reminder to all who pass by that you have dedicated a part of your home to the respite of tea. It is a way to say to both family and friends, "Come, take time to sit a spell; let's remind ourselves how much we love one another."

1. Measure the panels or areas on the screen that you want to cover. Copy these dimensions full sized onto the Kraft paper.

2. Experiment with the design of the various paper ephemera and trims you've collected to compose your collage. Overlap the images as desired, covering the panel areas as much as possible. Continue until you've covered the Kraft paper for each area of the screen you wish to decorate, making sure the overall look of these images suits you.

3. Once you're satisfied that these arrangements are your favorites, it's time to place the images onto the screen

*Step 1:*
*Copy the dimensions*
*of the panels onto Kraft paper.*

## design schemes

The Victorian style of overkill means you can really pack the images into your decoupage screen. However, that era also included some remarkably simple, clean designs you could duplicate — and if you want to do something wild and modern, go for it. I used the "crowded" Victorian style because that matched the style of most of my paper ephemera.

Questions to consider for the best design, no matter what the style, are:

- Do these images follow a theme?
- Do the items follow a color scheme?
- Is there any repetition that should be changed?
- Is there some trim, photo, or fabric that can be added to each of the panels to create continuity?
- Does any space look emptier or fuller than another?

panels. Carefully lay the Kraft paper with the images on the floor next to the screen. (If you have a Polaroid camera, take a few photos to guide you in the actual pasting process.)

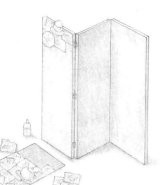

4. Remove the collage objects one at a time and paste them directly onto the screen, using your "layout" as a guide. The simplest way is to go from left to right, top to bottom. Apply rubber cement to the back of each object, being sure to cover all edges, then secure it firmly to the panel. Repeat until the panels are completed.

**Step 4:**
*Paste each collage item individually onto the screen.*

5. If any edges or pieces of wood show through, add ribbons, paper, or more images to cover.

6. Allow the glued papers to dry thoroughly, at least overnight.

7. Next, brush the entire assemblage with a clear varnish suitable for decoupage, painting it on in even strokes from left to right, then top to bottom.

**Step 7:**
*Brush the finished collage with clear varnish*

8. Allow the varnish to dry at least overnight.

# tea in the dining room

*Each tea hour must become a masterpiece to serve as a distillation of*
*all tea hours, as if it were the first and with no other to follow.*
*And so the act of drinking tea must be attended by beauty.*
— Lu Yu, *The Classic of Tea, Origins & Rituals* (780)

**t**he dining room of my childhood home was separate from the living room, and large enough for a polished mahogany table with at least six or eight matching chairs, a corner curio cabinet or two, and a buffet, atop which was set a sterling silver tea service, always at the ready. A breakfront protected and showed off the finer dinnerware we used for special occasions, including special teacups and saucers collected over the years.

I've had the pleasure of tea and company in many dining rooms, each with a special aura created by the owners that set the tone for a relaxing dinner hour. One such dining room was painted Williamsburg green, a soft pale green from the Revolutionary War period, framed with white-painted woodwork — a rare detail found only in older homes like this one, a Cape Cod frame house.

The dining room had a massive table with well-designed, carved chairs and a dramatic breakfront, and, of course, the shining silver tea set on the buffet. The room was sunny and bright and the scene for many birthday parties and other celebrations of coworkers of the hostess, a large gray-haired woman with a precision to her manners. This trait made her, in her youth, a marvelous secretary for the film company begun by actors Mary Pickford and Douglas Fairbanks, and continued into her alleged retirement, when she worked for the local newspaper where we first met.

Many times after she re-retired from the newspaper I would stop by for an afternoon cup of tea (she had gin) and we would laugh and talk about her family and mine, the changing neighborhood, our mutual friends, and, of course, the way lives turn out. She had the most amazing gift for starting and uplifting conversation of anyone I'd ever met. She was named Grace, a remarkable example of someone living up to her name.

Despite her supremely good manners, and despite her name (or because of it), Grace was also a bawdy lady, always game for embarrassing her grown children by retelling outrageous family anecdotes or for revealing rather intimate details of her life with her husband of more than 50 years. She was sometimes asked, "Ever think of divorcing Bob?" "Not likely," she would reply. "Murder, however, is a definite maybe."

Like Grace, my mother grew up in a family home with a huge dining room, the better to accommodate parents and seven children, a typical family in those days. My grandfather had a furniture store that sold rather ordinary beds, dining sets, and living room sofas and chairs, but in his house were handcarved wooden tables and chairs, and two massive Italian tables inlaid with exquisite mosaics. On top of these tables sat a brass carriage clock on one side and a metal samovar from Russia, complete with the manufacturer's details in Cyrillic script.

That carriage clock and the samovar are now part of the decor of my own dining room, a teak-walled, hardwood-floored, sunny room overlooking Richardson Bay. Here I can serve tea to friends at lunch or dinner, or sit quietly by myself in the dusk of day.

Each day varies, yet there is always something quite therapeutic about a regime that includes looking out at ducks swimming along or egrets stepping slowly with their ultralong, wire-thin legs over floating logs, or gulls swooping down for a quick snack of smelt. It's like having season tickets for the best ballet in town, performed anytime you enter my tearoom/dining room.

In the morning I can enjoy a brisk cup of Darjeeling while eating fresh fruits of the season and a toasted slice of delicious cranberry pumpkin bread.

*Formality is what most people associate with tea in the dining room, but this need not be the case for you.*

I've spent many hundreds of happy hours in my dining room with friends, and tea. I can remember celebratory afternoon teas of sandwiches, scones, and sweets with a different tea for each course, from a superb Ceylon to a fragrant passion fruit blend and a palate-cleansing Lung Ching green. Many friends have come for a drop-by cup of Assam with cubes of raw brown sugar and real whole milk, "just to talk." A laugh-filled dinner with best friends finished by rounds and rounds of the best Ti Kwan Yin oolong served *gung fu* style in tiny cups is one of my favorite memories. And then there were the instances of lingering past the time to say good night with that special someone, as we watched the dance of the Silver Needle white tea in a glass.

Being able to serve a meal, simple or elaborate, in a room dedicated to fine dining is not as common as it once was. Many homes and apartments do not have a separate room for dining, merely an area that is part of the living room. Still, you can recapture that feeling of a dedicated space by using interior design solutions that combine function with an artful form of celebrating and displaying your treasured tea things.

## COLLECTING AND DECORATING WITH TEAWARE

The choices of how to display tea accessories are only limited by your imagination, but you probably already have a few places in your dining room or dining area that can serve as an elegant backdrop for your tea

*An arrangement of teapots, cups, and accessories can liven up an empty shelf.*

things. Tabletop curio cabinets, floor-standing cabinets or breakfronts, lighted areas of bookcases, glass-paneled or open cabinetry, and on top of the dining table itself are all options.

I have a bookcase in my dining room that is a mini gallery of my "tea art." The bottom two shelves are packed with my beloved tea books, and the top three shelves display a mélange of whimsical teapots and traditional tea-for-two sets for drop-in guests. In the corner is a tea cart on which I keep my electric teakettle, water filter jug, and a tray. I change the teapots and accessories constantly, matching the pot to the type of tea, or matching cups and pots to the type of tea service.

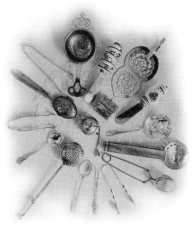

*A mix of antique and contemporary spoons, forks, strainers, tongs, spreaders, and infusers create a unique design.*

Looking at or handling an object of art is an enriching, satisfying experience, one to be encouraged in every aspect of our lives. Fortunately for us tea lovers, the availability of pretty things for making tea affords us the everyday luxury of having tea with accoutrements that are as attractive as they are functional.

Whether your collection is a mixture of Chinese, Japanese, and European, or focuses on a particular material like silver, porcelain, or Yixing, show off its beauty. Today is the time to use your most treasured tea things, not "later" or for "special occasions." Every day that you can have tea is a special occasion. Who deserves it better than you?

Part of the joy of collecting is learning about why and how these utensils came to be, and another part is viewing them as works of art. Mote spoons, tea balls, strainers, slop bowls, teaspoons, lemon forks, teatime silverware, and all the other enchanting tea table collectibles are both beautiful to look at and remarkably useful. These accessories can enhance your private and social tea experiences, add sophistication to the interior design of your home, and become a natural part of living the tea life. From a variety of cultures come pots and cups and utensils that are ornate or refined, elaborate or supremely functional; all are art to use with your daily tea. Learning a little of their history helps you appreciate how clever tea lovers were to create such timeless pieces.

## Collectible Teapots

Perhaps no tea-related collectible is as popular as the teapot. The birthplace of the teapot, the Yixing province of China, has been the source for thousands of masterfully designed teapots made of an incredibly fine clay. Remarkably, many antique porcelain and Yixing pots remain, now found in museums throughout the world, graceful reminders of how classic designs and exceptional craftsmanship can turn a utilitarian object into a work of art.

*This highly collectible Yixing pot is both beautiful and functional.*

After China shared its secrets for porcelain making, Great Britain developed an entire industry devoted to fine "china," which has lasted to the present day. Gilded, painted, gracefully shaped, these pots are indeed fine works of art. Both the Yixing and the porcelain teapot come in an enormous range of styles from elegant to severely simple; some re-create animals, fruits, vegetables, or people. They all pour tea into a cup and bring a smile or a sense of beauty to tea drinkers every time they're used.

## DISPLAYING YOUR TEA TREASURES

It has been my basic philosophy over the past few years that "one is an item, two is a set, three is a collection — and usually requires an effort to dust." When I realize I have three of something, an alarm goes off in my head and I put on the brakes. Very few people I know, even tea lovers, have my resolve, or my lack of floor space. I can, however, appreciate carefully amassed collections of things people love, and admire the amazingly resourceful and innovative ways tea friends have discovered to display their treasures. Here are some possible collectibles and favorite techniques for their display.

## *Tea Caddies*

The best place to keep tea is in a canister of heavy porcelain, metal, or glass, with a tight-fitting lid, stored in a dark, cool place to keep the tea fresh. Decorative tea caddies are best used to hold the leaves during the tea hour; a host can use one to measure out the tea and put it in the teapot or other vessel. Guests will certainly find a well-crafted wood or ceramic caddy prettier to look at than a tin can with a glaring label on it. Immediately after the tea hour, the remaining tea leaves should be emptied from the caddy and replaced into the original canister or a storage jar.

**Chinese caddies.** The original Chinese caddies were often made in either square or hexagonal shapes. However, contemporary Chinese tea caddies, particularly Yixing pottery caddies, come in the same charming shapes as many of the teapots that are a delight to the eye of any collector.

The famous "purple sand" color of Yixing clay is the most popular, but other colors are available: green, terra-cotta, ecru, teal, and black. As with American or European tea caddies, immediately after a tea, any tea leaves remaining in a Yixing caddy should be emptied into the canister.

**Japanese caddies.** Japanese caddies are small, and made of the exquisite woods so important to that culture. Many high-quality tea caddies are considered so significant to the Japanese that they are handed down from generation to generation as precious heirlooms.

During *chanoyu,* the formal tea ceremony, it is not unusual for a caddy to be passed around for the guests to openly admire it, even turning it over to read the mark of the artist or designer. Japanese

*A classic Chinese Yixing caddy with a delicate nature motif.*

*A lovely Japanese-style caddy with Asian artwork.*

*Intricate paper inlays grace this antique wood British caddy.*

*This silver contemporary caddy shows a distintictly European flair.*

caddies are widely available, from modestly priced tins and wooden jars to one-of-a-kind caddies of rare woods and fine workmanship costing hundreds of dollars. They are artfully produced in every price range, and make exquisite additions to anyone's collection.

**British caddies.** In the hands of England's superior 18th-century cabinetmakers, tea caddies evolved from the ancient hexagonal Chinese shapes to rectangular boxes, with all the detailing of furniture making of that era. The portable boxes could easily be carried from room to room. But others, called teapoys, were built onto three-legged stands and quickly became sought-after pieces of furniture for the homes of the wealthy.

Inside these caddies, often made of polished woods with fine detailing, were three compartments: Two held different choices of tea, and the third was used for blending. Sugar, a dearly expensive and still-novel condiment in the mid-1800s, was often kept in the third container, and under lock and key.

Some British caddies had one or two compartments, for green and black teas, and most compartments were made of metal, or from the same wood as the caddy itself. Others contained glistening cut-glass bowls for the sugar. The variety and workmanship were endless and fabulous; indeed, these caddies are so highly collectible — and expensive — today because of their stunning marriage of craft and art.

**Contemporary caddies.** Contemporary American caddies, lovely reproductions of European styles, are affordably priced and come in a variety of styles and materials. Silver plate caddies are a beautiful addition to the tea table, but they should not be used for long periods of time because the metal can interact with the tea. Instead, use them only during the actual tea service as a pretty accessory to the table. Promptly remove the unused leaves when you're done, and replace them in the original canister or storage jar.

## Teapots

You bought another one, didn't you? Well, who could blame you? It's adorable! It's gorgeous! It completes a set! Whatever the reason, if your heart says yes, then add another teapot to your collection. Unless your collection is so large it requires building on another room, or starting your own teapot museum, consider some of these ideas for displaying and using your beloved teapots.

- Place your good dinnerware in padded storage bags and into an available closet to free up your breakfront for displaying your pretty teapots and accessories.

- Find a wooden step stool, paint it a color that coordinates with the walls or varnish it in a nice wood tone to go with your furnishings, and set teapots on each step. This is particularly fetching if you have a library stepladder with steps on both sides.

*An unused step stool is the perfect place for your teapot collection.*

- Make your teapots, especially those orphaned without a lid, multifunctional by using them to store utensils such as wooden spoons, pencils and pens, remote controls, eyeglasses, or sewing notions. If a pot still has its lid, simply rest the lid against the pot, on its side. They're also delightful vases for flowers.

- Fill teapots with pasta, rice, or beans and use them as bookends for your cookbooks in the kitchen, or for your collection of books on tea. If you're concerned about pests, place a bay leaf in with the grains, or if you prefer, use sawdust, sand, or gravel instead of grains.

## Teacups

To me, a teacup is a superb combination of all the ceramic arts — sculpture, painting, and glazing — as well as superb function following a graceful form. Holding a beautifully designed cup, feeling the warmth of the hot tea within it, and touching the silky smoothness of the glaze all contribute to the gentility of time spent over tea.

Once, while I interviewed an elderly woman (then age 91) about her role in the growth of her neighborhood, she offered my photographer and me a cup of tea. Our concerns that we were taxing her strength were quickly put to rest as she gracefully got up before we could extend our arms in assistance, shooed us away, and walked slowly into her kitchen, as spotless as the rest of the house. It was a reminder to us of her continuing ability to care for herself and her things.

She talked to us amid the tinkling of cups and whistling of the kettle, then slowly she walked back to the living room, somehow balancing three servings of tea on a tray with regulation sugar and creamer. The cups were exquisite. The photographer's cup was a smooth, soft, creamy white, with deep matching curves on both cup and saucer that looked like Issey Miyake or Fortuny fabric pleats.

Mine was a lavender, pink, and gold confection; the cup stood on three miniature legs and held a variegated bouquet of posies in its bowl that I only discovered when I had finished drinking the tea. The cup stood gracefully in a saucer that curved up high to hold it securely in place. Our hostess drank from an iridescent lusterware cup of blue and peach, so thin the sun streamed through it as she lifted the cup to her lips.

We continued our interview, took a few photos of our hostess, and bade our good-byes, marveling at how such a simple experience — having tea — made us both feel we had played hooky instead of working. I wrote up the story, including details of the woman's family history and her continuing independent lifestyle. The story was printed the next day and the newspaper got a flood of letters, not about the woman's role in the history of her little town, nor her countless hours of volunteer effort for the library her family had founded generations ago, but in response to my descriptions of our little tea respite.

That experience, some 15 years ago, has stayed with me. Now, every time I see a pretty teacup, I think of the elegant old woman and her gift to us, sharing an artful cup of tea.

Teacups come in such amazingly different designs, in various sizes and shapes, with and without handles, with and without saucers. Teacups are probably the easiest collectible to amass because so many exist, both antique and contemporary. They can be matched to your tea, to your mood, to your guests.

*There are a variety of options for teaware display.*

In the 18th century cups were handleless; they came with a flat saucer on which they were placed, and a curved saucer into which the tea was poured. It was considered customary then to drink from this saucer. Asian cups are still handleless, and some cultures even drink tea from glasses encased in pretty metal holders.

One of the dearest ways to collect teacups in the southern United States is for girlfriends to give a bride a teacup when attending a bridal shower. This provides the newlywed with an immediate collection, and every time friends stop by for tea, they can use "their" cups.

Have more than two sets of cups and saucers? Would you like to show off a particularly exquisite cup and saucer set? How should you display them? There are a variety of options for teaware display but here are a few suggestions:

*Stacking your teacups provides the ideal solution to the problem of display space limitations.*

*A commercial teacup stand is a graceful, safe option for teaware showcasing.*

**Stack 'em.** One friend of mine literally stacks her cups on top of one another — saucer, cup, saucer, cup — and puts them all over the lower ledge of her fireplace, and on her windowsill. I still hold my breath every time I visit, but she swears there has never been a catastrophe.

**Stand 'em on their own.** Commercial teacup stands are readily available at any hardware or homeware store. You place the cup upright into the round bottom depression and place the saucer on its edge, both to show off the potter's design. These come in black, rosewood, or light woods, and can accommodate cups and saucers of all sizes. Any flat surface is perfect for a teacup stand: end tables, mantels, ledges, breakfronts or curio cabinets, or even dressers, wide windowsills, bookcases, and any nook and cranny that's out of reach of little children or careless grown-ups.

**Hang 'em up.** Also from the hardware store are brass brackets with springs to hold up plates and saucers on the wall or shelf. Use cup hooks to display cups from the ceilings of cabinets, and free up a lot of space in the bargain.

## Creative Ideas for Using Teacups and Saucers

If you're fresh out of ideas for ways to use and display your teacup collection, try some of these practical tips:

- Sturdy commercial teacups make good votive holders. If you're a candle maker, fill up the cups with beeswax and a wick, and you've got a pretty candle and holder in one. Glue the cup to the saucer and you have a lovely hostess gift.

- Instead of plopping the car and house keys down on a shelf or possibly scratching a table, put them in an old teacup. If you use a brightly colored cup, everyone in the household will notice it — and the keys.

- Place a cup in the bathroom to hold cotton swabs, and one in the kitchen for toothpicks or to hold your rings when you remove them to cook or wash.

- Saving coins for the laundry or the bus? Place a cup and saucer on the dresser for change. It's a lot nicer to look at a pretty cup than at a pile of coins spread out everywhere.

- Mugs make good silverware caddies or pencil holders when not used for their primary purpose.

## Paper Ephemera on Tea

The history of the world of tea can be traced through paper ephemera — all those images from packaging, promotional items, and contemporary advertisements for tea. The most ethereal, and most costly, are the hand-calligraphied scrolls created exclusively for Japanese teahouses, with poems and illustrations that both the Chinese and the Japanese artists have created through the ages on the nature of tea.

Tea tags and tea bag envelopes are very accessible, inexpensive, and easy to collect. They began as an advertising gimmick in the early 1920s when that cleverest of tea entrepreneurs, Sir Thomas Lipton, first realized that a tag on a tea bag could serve two functions: It could help customers infuse the tea without needing a spoon or fingers to pick the bag out of the cup, and its blank space could be used to advertise Sir Thomas' "Ceylon tea." Other tea blenders soon followed suit, adding such creative touches as pithy sayings, pretty pictures, and decorative graphics, all of which now provide collectors with a miniature version of the evolution of type printing and advertising in the 20th century. Of course, rare and unusual tea tags and tea bag envelopes are the most highly valued of these collectibles.

*Many tea bag envelopes and tea tags are printed with striking images or poetic phrases.*

LEVEL OF EXPERTISE:
medium

TOOLS AND MATERIALS:
ledge

stepladder

paint or stain

brush

decorative trims, fabrics, papers, rubber stamps — whatever you'd like to incorporate in your teapot display

teapots and/or any other tea accessories you'd like to display

fixative (one brand to look for in the hardware store is Quake-wax, but there are many others)

## TEA ACCESSORIES DISPLAY LEDGE

An idea that is both space saving and flexible is to place a ledge all around your dining room or dining area, 1 foot or more from the ceiling. You can then decorate the ledge in any way you like — perhaps with your favorite tea-themed cutouts or contact paper — and use it to display your teapot collection.

If you have experience with carpentry, you can install such a ledge yourself. If not, you should be able to find a local carpenter or handyperson to help you out; you might also look for books on basic carpentry skills. Just remember that your ledge will be located over people's heads and hold fragile, and/or heavy crockery. It's important that it be installed correctly and safely! Also, if you prefer, you can use the instructions below to turn any existing shelf or ledge in your home into a teapot display.

As a Californian, I'm always concerned about objects falling off shelves during earthquakes, but you don't need to be on a fault line to protect your pots. If you have rambunctious pets, children, or lots of activity in your house, it makes sense to be protective about your collectibles. For this reason, I recommend anchoring your accessories to the ledge with a fixative.

The ledge can also accommodate related or even contrasting items such as unusual plates, silver or decorative trays, cozies, dolls, small paintings or drawings of tea accoutrements, dried wreaths or flowers, pretty books, or anything else you love to coordinate or contrast with your teapot collection.

1. Decide how you'd like to finish your ledge — with paint, with stain, with decorative trim, and so on. Here are some of your choices:

- Keep the ledge unfinished (a clear finish can be used to protect the wood while retaining the unfinished look).

- Keep the ledge unfinished, but add accents. For example, you can decorate the front of the ledge with a paper shelf trim of cutout lace or a preprinted pattern. If your teapots are primarily plain colors, a printed pattern offers a nice contrast. If the pots are a riot of pattern, use a plain or lace paper in a color that matches your walls to add the finishing touch that sets off the shelf. Another option for shelf trimming is tea-themed rubber stamps, which are dipped in paint and "stamped" on paper. The paper is then glued or tacked to the ledge. Or, use tea-themed stencils to paint directly on the edge of the wood.

## selecting the ledge

If you are an experienced carpenter you can certainly make your own, but the choices of ready-made ledges are so spectacular, why not choose from these? Ready-made ledges even come with grooves for secure plate display. If the ledge you choose is decorative, that will be part of its charm. They add detailing and design interest in addition to their function as a place to put your teapots. Styles are varied from gingerbread details to western railings, from sleek elegant styles to the most baroque carvings.

You can have an employee at the hardware store or lumberyard saw the ledge into the sizes you need to fit each wall; this step saves time and money, especially if you do not own a saw. The craftsmen at the lumberyard or hardware store measure and cut every day, so rely on their expertise.

## breakfast tea

A breakfast tea is a wonderful way to start off the day, especially those special holiday Mondays, first days of school or a new job, or birthday celebrations.

Much of the preparation can be done the night before. Set the table with plates, flatware, teacups, cloth napkins, and place mats or tablecloth. For a wintertime breakfast tea, candles will add enough light, and a soft ease into the day.

Organize platters and serving pieces. Check that all the ingredients are available for the menu. Create a centerpiece of stacks of teacups and saucers for everyone to take one off the stack as they arrive.

- Omelets, plain or with herbs
- Fresh fruit in season
- Braided bread
- Assorted jams and curds, sweet butter, and/or peanut butter
- Assam tea

- Stain the ledge to a tone that will either complement or match existing wood furniture in the room.

- Paint the ledge to match or contrast with the walls of the room.

2. Wait for the ledge to dry; this is very important! Most will need at least four hours to dry. Always read the product label!

3. Bring out your tea accessories collection and place the items around the room, on the floor against each wall. This will give you a good idea of placement by size, color, shape, and style.

4. After you have arranged your accessories to suit you, place your tea things on the ledge. Have a pal help you out (offer tea as a reward, of course!): One of you can hand up the teapots while the other places them on the ledge.

5. Apply a fixative to the bottom of each item before its final placement to ensure more solid positioning.

**Step 4:** *Arrange your tea items on the ledge.*

# tea in the office

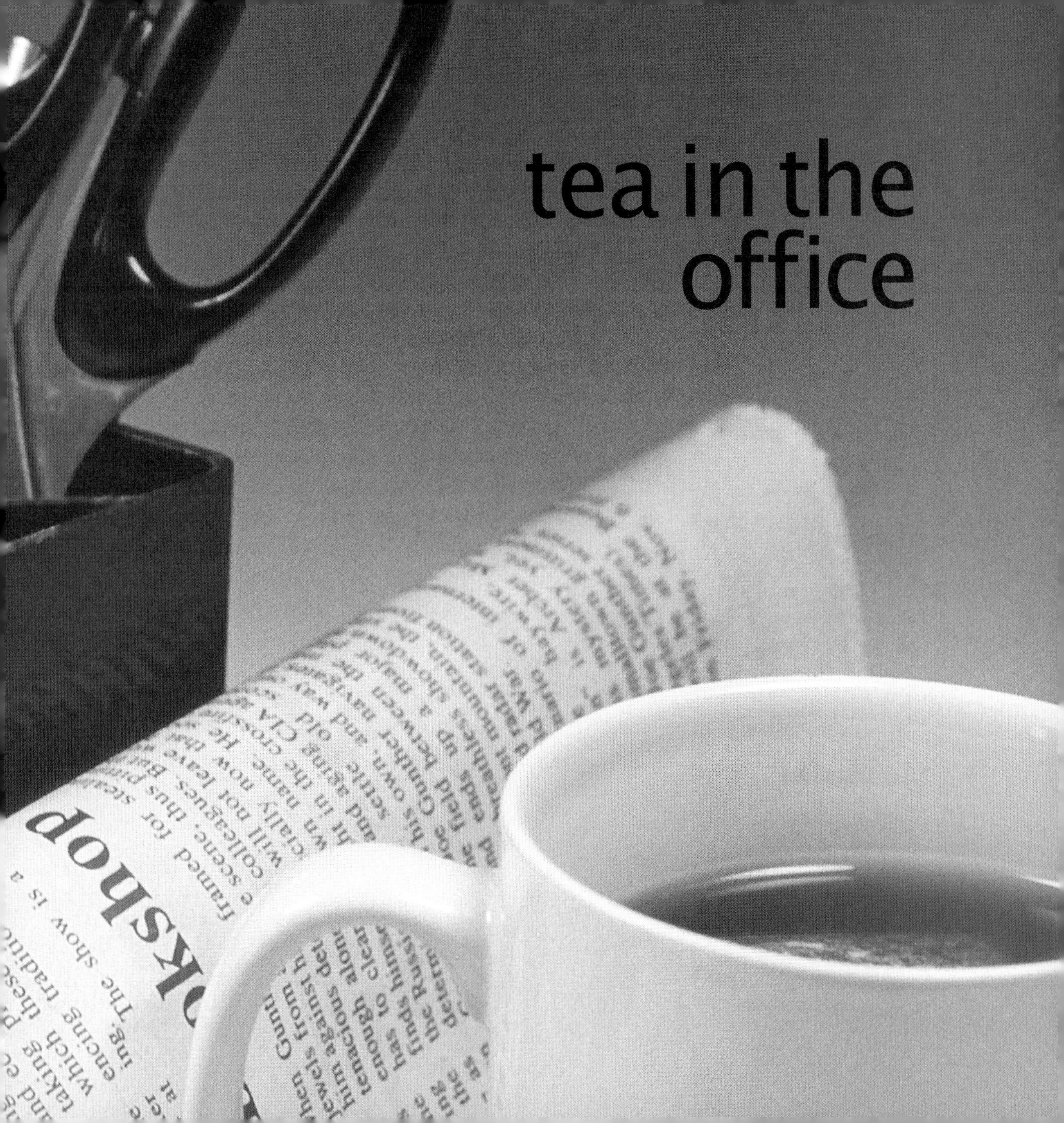

Whether you're the employee or the employer, it's
important that you take a break during the work-
day. Another phone call to take, another client to
meet, another letter to answer can be detours
from your much-needed respite — the daily tea
break. Instead of allowing such diversions to interrupt, make a commitment to yourself to set aside the same time every day for tea,
11 A.M., or 4 P.M., or anytime you choose. Stick to it. Let everyone know
that's your teatime.

## TEA IN THE BUSINESS OFFICE

Think you can't bring one more thing into the
shop or office? Think again. You can store
your tea things in a tackle box, Shaker box,
unused wastebasket, or unused briefcase.
Did you know that 80 percent of all filed
papers are never referred to a second time?
That's reason enough to consider using the
filing cabinet or largest drawer in

*Store your tea things in a
Shaker box and tuck it out of
the way when not in use.*

your desk for your tea things. Bring a thermos of hot water to work if
you can't get hot water from the water cooler or if there truly is no room
for an electric kettle.

If you have your own office, close the door. If you don't have a door,
get a screen or partition. Hang out a DO NOT DISTURB sign. Refuse to
answer any requests except genuine emergencies.

Get out that thermos of hot water, put the tea bag in your cup or the tea in your pot, and make yourself a pleasure. Make time for tea; it will pay you back in refreshment, clarity of thought, and renewed vigor to complete the work ahead of you.

Before you know it, your colleagues will not only get the hint and leave you alone for your 10 minutes of teatime, they'll start making their own space and time for tea.

## TEA SPOTS IN THE HOME OFFICE

Any small corner in the home office can be a spot for tea. Here are a number of ideas for creating your special place:

- Use a drawer or two in a vanity table or bureau
- Create a little haven under a stairwell
- Eliminate the hall closet for clothing and make it your tea spot
- Use a drawer in your desk, or make the end table next to your bed a tea spot storage unit

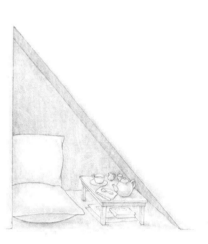

*Even the small space under a stairwell can be used as a private tea spot.*

This is dedicated space; be territorial about it. Books, clothes, nonfunctional decorative pieces, even linens can go somewhere else; it's more important to make space — and time — for tea. If there really is no room, consider the following ideas:

- Paint a step stool, place your tea things on each rung, and set it out on perpetual display to be accessible — and to remind you to stop a moment for tea
- Clear off some books in bookcases for your tea things
- Use a cedar chest, decorative trunk, or another boxlike piece of furniture to store your accessories. It will double as a tabletop
- If your home office is in the kitchen, maintain a dedicated corner just for "tea and thee"

## BREWING THE PERFECT CUP IN THE OFFICE

Everyone who drinks tea over a length of time becomes rather territorial about their favorite paraphernalia, and it's easy to believe that yours is the best way to brew tea. I am no exception. I actually have four favorites, two for solo enjoyment and two for company.

### Sharing with Office Friends

For colleagues who will take tea with you, the Jenaer Glassworks teapot is terrific. It is clear glass which shows off the beautiful color of the brewed tea and its gold filter is easy to remove to avoid overbrewing (and it's easy to rinse clean, too). Best of all, its slight indentation at the end of the spout guarantees dripless pouring.

A similar filter principle is used by my other three favorite teapots: the Chatsford, the Swiss Gold Filter, and The Tea-One Brew™. The Chatsford is a British-made teapot of heavy porcelain available in all the bright primary colors, plus black or white. Its classic red plastic and metal mesh filter captures the leaves and makes removing them neat and simple. The pots are available in sizes for two, four, and six, so you'll find a pot that's perfect for any group or solo tea pleasure.

*A combination teapot and cup saves space in an otherwise crowded office.*

### Solo Tea

For tea for one, I would recommend either the Swiss Gold Filter for Tea or The Tea-One Brew™. The Swiss Gold Filter (also available for that other beverage, coffee) sits right on top of your tea cup or mug. Place your leaves in the filter, and pour in the hot water. The water steeps through the leaves into the cup, and makes a perfect single cup every time.

The Tea-One Brew™ is a terrific combination of clear vessel and a French-press-style filter that keeps the tea leaves away from the liquid. It also comes with a lid that serves as a coaster for holding the filter. To re-infuse, simply place the filter back into the vessel, pour on more water, allow to brew, press the "magic" button, and the brewed tea pours down into the bottom of the vessel. This particular pot makes excellent tea no matter the variety; from delicate white and green to heartier oolong and black.

The benefit of all these teapots is the ease in which loose leaf teas can be brewed in filters that can be removed with equal ease. Many of the catalogs listed in Resources, in addition to high-quality tea shops, cook shops, and gift catalogs, carry one or all of these teapots. The Jenaer Glassworks teapot is even a Metropolitan Museum of Art design winner and a staple in its gift catalogs and shops.

## The Perfect Water

What about water? The ideal way to brew the freshest pot or cup of tea is to keep bottled spring water on hand (if you don't have a water cooler) and heat up the water in an electric kettle.

Generally, the hot water in water coolers will do quite well, but if you have your own favorite bottled waters or you live in a city with great tap water, invest in a good-quality stainless steel Thermos bottle. You can fill it up at home and bring it with you to the office and the Thermos bottle will keep the water hot for hours. When you're ready for tea, open up the Thermos bottle, pour out the water needed, brew for the length of time you prefer, and voilá, perfect tea in the office.

## Condiments and Snacks

If your office has the benefit of a kitchen or even a small refrigerator, you can keep milk there. Or, keep packages of powdered milk, sugar, and sugar substitutes in your "tea spot" and they'll be ready for your tea whenever you are.

As for snacks, baking at the office or shop might not be all that convenient (but wouldn't it smell lovely?) but packaged cookies, biscuits, cheese, and crackers, are easy to keep around for when that "sinking

time was when I could 'ave a nice cuppa with me mates, the rest 'o the cleaners, sit in comfort in a room they give us, put me feet up and 'ave a bit of gossip. Now I keeps me tea things in the broom cupboard and 'as to make do with sittin' on the stairs by me lonesome, but still, tea's tea.

— JEANNE M. DAMS,
*Trouble in the Town Hall*
(1996)

feeling" hits you. Keep food fresh by putting opened packages of crackers in large plastic bags that can be sealed tightly, or, if you have one, put them in the refrigerator along with cheeses or other perishables. Fresh fruits are great, too, so pack up some for the office and enjoy them with your tea.

### No-Hassle Cleanup

Worried about what to do with the used tea leaves? If there are plants in the office, just spread them evenly around the dirt. If not, dump the leaves into a paper towel, and toss them in the garbage. If you use tea bags, simply wrap them in a paper towel and discard in the garbage, or put them in the refridgerator. The next time you feel eyestrain from the computer, take out the cooled teabags and put them on your eyelids for a few minutes.

## portable "tea spot"

Consider creating a portable "tea spot," such as a good-sized basket, wedding basket, or hat box, and keeping it in a closet. Or, take it with you wherever you go. It can hold a Thermos of pre-heated water, a box of tea, a teapot and cup combo, a spoon, and a ceramic bowl to keep spent leaves. That's it.

To use, put in a spoonful of tea and heated water into the pot and steep. Pour tea into the cup and enjoy. Can't drink tea without milk and sugar? Keep restaurant-style packages of sugar and creamer. Now you have no excuses to go without your tea and, more important, your tea break. (Of course, if you have more room, you can always store a bottle of spring water and an electric teakettle.)

# tea in the
# kitchen

*No matter where I put my guests,*
*they seem to like my kitchen best.*
— TRADITIONAL SAYING

just the word *kitchen* can take me back to the yellow Formica and chrome table where our family gathered every evening for dinner and to talk about our days. Our kitchen had blue linoleum and was quite large, about 20 feet by 30 feet — perfect for roller skating. Of course, skating was not allowed in the house, but that didn't stop my sister and me, although the curved thresholds at each doorway sometimes tripped us up.

The kitchen was always warm with the smell of a mammoth pot of tomato sauce cooking for hours, steaming up the windows that overlooked the flamboyant apple tree in the backyard. Or the floating fragrance of Toll House cookies perfectly mated with cups of mostly milk with a dollop of hot black tea. As we got older the proportions of milk to tea changed, but fortunately the cookies remained the same.

Occasionally, the kitchen table was used for Girl Scout projects or various gifts and cards we would make for holidays. My mother would sit with my sister and me, telling us stories as we learned sewing, mending, embroidery, and other handiwork skills together.

## Choosing the Perfect Tea

No matter how small or large, or how simple or elaborate, the kitchen seems to beckon us to share all of life's good things. For many families, the kitchen table is the place where couples balance the budget, friends chat about their lives, and children do their homework while dinner is being prepared. It's also the obvious place for any "family chef" to sit down for a few minutes to sip a good cup of tea to relax and reenergize before finishing the job. The kitchen is a versatile room, and your choices can be, too.

Any tea that you love is a great tea to drink, but I find that one of the pleasures of tea drinking is selecting something hearty or mild, sweet or astringent, to match my mood. And the best place to have a cup is the coziness of a kitchen redolent with the smells of the next meal being prepared, or freshly scrubbed after a big cooking project.

Among the teas I enjoy drinking while cooking or cleaning in my kitchen is pu-erh, the aged digestive tea of mainland China. An all-day tea, it is also so flavorful that you can reinfuse it several times during the day and never have too weak a cup.

## Using Your Creativity

While heating the water for your tea, consider the many decorative touches you can add to the kitchen from tea-themed wallpaper, linen dishcloths and washcloths, pot holders and aprons, refrigerator magnets, and prints, watercolors, and other artwork for the walls that depict teacups and teapots. And the pots and cups themselves always add a colorful touch to any kitchen. Be bold. Be adventurous. Spread your collection around for its visual charms.

The following projects are easy to assemble on the kitchen table, and can be used to decorate the kitchen or any other part of the house. After that, I present some creative ideas for using tea as a condiment — yes, *cooking* with tea.

Fine chefs at five-star hotels and restaurants and innovative cooks everywhere are experimenting with baking and cooking with tea. Tea adds a savory bite or delicate fragrance to many dishes. Best of all, tea adds flavor without adding calories. You can concoct mouth-watering beef, chicken, fish, or vegetable dishes or rejuvenate last night's leftovers with tea. All you really need is the tea, a few simple ingredients, and a creative spirit.

## brewing pu-erh

Pu-erh is a marvelous tea on many levels: it's difficult to overbrew, it can be re-infused several times, it's a digestive, and is excellent to drink at nighttime because it has very little caffeine. Best of all, it's richly satisfying, with a hearty flavor that makes it an ideal tea for those who want to make the segue from coffee to tea.

It is also the only intentionally-aged tea; some as old as 50 years. Often called the Chinese penicillin, it appears to have many beneficial bacteria in it, which probably account for its distinctive musty aroma and taste.

To brew pu-erh, take about 1 teaspoon of the leaves and put them in your cup or mug. Pour boiling water over the leaves. This is one of the few teas that must be brewed with boiling water to help activate the tea's positive bacteria. Brew for at least two or three minutes, decant, and drink. It can be re-infused, depending on its quality, up to three imes, and can be brewed longer if you like a very intense taste. Drink pu-erh plain.

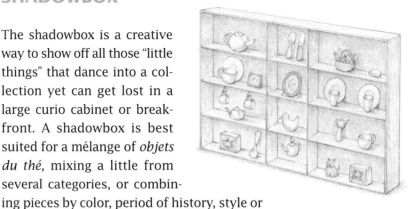

## SHADOWBOX

LEVEL OF EXPERTISE:
medium; some dexterity
  involved

TOOLS AND MATERIALS:
preassembled shadowbox

sandpaper

stain or paint

paintbrush

tea collectibles

fabric or paper (contact
  paper or wallpaper are
  best) to cover the box

ruler or measuring tape

scissors

glue (Elmer's or other wood-
  suitable adhesive)

X-acto knife

lace, ribbon, buttons, or any
  other decorative touch

cup hooks

screwdriver and screws for
  hanging

wire for hanging (optional)

hooks for hanging (optional)

The shadowbox is a creative way to show off all those "little things" that dance into a collection yet can get lost in a large curio cabinet or breakfront. A shadowbox is best suited for a mélange of *objets du thé,* mixing a little from several categories, or combining pieces by color, period of history, style or culture, or similar classification. Small size is your only requirement, because most shadowboxes hold only small objects. Because this project uses objects you're sure to find around the house, it's easy to make a simple shadowbox without a lot of expense.

You can make a shadowbox for miniature teapots or teacups, sugar tongs, and small strainers. Check out dollhouse stores for tea-related accessories. Consider making a shadowbox with tea-themed jewelry to house your pins, bracelets, earrings, or cufflinks. Hang the jewelry on cup hooks or simply lay the pieces flat on the "shelves" of the shadowbox.

How about a box to hold postage stamps and tea-themed postcards or stationery, or those rubber stamps you use (or not) to make tea impressions on paper or fabric? Perhaps you'd like to include objects that remind you of your favorite tea experiences or companions. For example: antique or modern tea tins, tea invitations, stickers, photos of you and friends enjoying tea, pretty tea bag envelopes or tea tags, tea salon menus or business cards, or even teatime recipes.

If there's room, a shadowbox would look nice on top of the refrigerator, along with your cookbooks on their shelves, or in place of some dishes in a glass-fronted cabinet in the kitchen or pantry. Or hang the shadowbox on the kitchen wall, or place it on the wall behind the counter, and you'll have a piece of tea whimsy to glance at any time you enter the kitchen.

1. Using a preassembled box, smooth any rough edges with sandpaper and brush clean.

2. Stain or paint the outside, following the manufacturer's directions.

3. If you're covering the box's interior with fabric or paper, measure each shelf and measure the inside area behind the shelves. Also, measure the outside if you want to cover that area with fabric or paper.

## selecting a shadowbox

Premade shadowboxes are available at most arts and crafts stores, and ready-made deep picture frames are easy to convert into shadowboxes. Most shadowboxes are a light plywood or similar material, so if you'd like a more finished look, it's best to either stain them, paint them, or cover them with paper or fabric. This do-it-yourself project works well with any good cotton, linen, or burlap. Silk or velvet would add a touch of elegance, but for all fabrics, choose a plain color or a pale pattern like a damask so that your objects will not be overwhelmed.

For an antique look, try using an old letterpress printer's drawer. These can be found in secondhand stores and antiques shops, and will add an old-time charm to your collectibles.

**Step 4:** *Glue fabric onto shelves and cut of the excess.*

4. With the scissors, cut out the fabric or paper to fit. Using glue, carefully paste in the fabric or paper where you want it. With an X-acto knife, trim the edges of the fabric evenly with the edge of the shelf or sides of the box. Cover the exposed edges with ribbon, lace, paint, or contrasting fabric. Allow several minutes for the glue to dry.

5. Gather your collectibles and arrange them on the shelves of the shadowbox until they suit your eye. Take a Polaroid shot of your placement, or carefully line your objects on a table, matching the placement, left to right, row by row.

6. If you're hanging any items, tap a small nail hole. Using your fingers, screw cup hooks into the hole on the interior "ceiling" of the shadowbox.

7. Place the selected items in the spots identified for each. They can be permanently placed by lightly gluing them all in the positions you selected earlier. Allow to dry overnight.

**Step 7:** *Use glue to permanently anchor the collectibles in the shadowbox.*

8. If you're hanging your shadowbox, install the hooks on the back of the shadowbox in the wall. Follow the manufacturer's insert for complete instructions. Install any necessary wall hoops or hooks, and hang the shadowbox in the desired place on the wall.

## CLEANING AND OTHER
## HOUSEHOLD HINTS

Leftover tea is a particularly versatile resource for many household tasks. Its deodorizing capabilities make it excellent to use alone or diluted with water for refreshing fabrics, straw mats, or cups, glasses, and pots that have stayed way too long in the cupboard. To avoid dyeing the fabric with the liquor, pour *through* the fabric to clean. Then, rinse thoroughly with hot water.

Putting spent tea leaves through the garbage disposal is as effective as a used lemon or baking soda to keep this germ catcher smelling fresh. Used leaves also work for a few days as an odor catcher in the refrigerator. Simply put the leaves on a small saucer, place on a refrigerator shelf, and let them do their magic.

**Bathe new furniture with tea.** Some new furniture comes with a light lacquer or coating to protect it from scratches when it's being moved from the showroom floor to your home. To eliminate the coating, steep five tea bags of black tea in 2 quarts warm water for about 20 minutes. Then dampen a clean, soft flannel cloth in the tea bath, squeeze out the excess, and wash down the furniture. With a second soft flannel cloth, wipe thoroughly dry. Apply furniture polish or wax only upon manufacturer's directions.

**Clean woks and skillets with tea.** It's quite common in Chinese restaurants and in the homes of Chinese cooks to use leftover pu-erh tea to clean the wok. Pu-erh, an intentionally aged Chinese tea, has fat-cutting properties that are legendary; perhaps that's why it's called the "cholesterol cutter." It does stand to reason that if pu-erh can aid digestion after meals, it can also wash away grease in a pan. Simply pour the tea liquor into the wok or pan and wipe off with a paper towel. The truth of its effectiveness will be on the towel. Repeat as necessary, then rinse the pan with clear water and wipe dry.

To double the effectiveness of your pet's flea powder, add crushed dried tea leaves. Take 1 cup green tea, such as Gunpowder, and crush the leaves, releasing the aroma and the natural oils. Mix thoroughly with 1 cup flea powder and sprinkle on your pet's bed or directly onto your pet, per the powder manufacturer's directions. The tea can also be used directly, without flea powder.

**Remove tea stains.** Every tea lover has his or her own technique for removing tea stains, but the most effective one I've ever tried comes from Mary Fry of Pasadena's Rose Tree Cottage. Mary's recipe is ⅛ cup powdered Biz combined with ¼ cup powdered Tide with Clorox. I've tried other dry bleaches and detergents, but I must admit these two together do the job best for me.

Pour water into a tub, then add the detergents and stir. Place your tea-stained napery inside, and allow to soak for about a half hour, or longer if the stains are old or very dark. Rinse thoroughly with clear water and hang outside to dry. You can rewash the fabric, again with the detergent, this time in the washing machine.

Another method for removing tea stains is to use ½ cup Biz alone in a sink of water; soak the cloth for three days. Then wash as normal with a detergent in the washing machine.

A third version of this stain-removal recipe is a bath of ½ cup white vinegar in 2 quarts water. Soak linens for 20 minutes; remove but do not rinse. Dry outside on the grass, if possible, or hang on a line. The combination of sunlight and vinegar will whiten the napery considerably without the harshness of bleach.

## COOKING WITH TEA

For centuries the Chinese have been cooking with tea, and tea-flavored dishes occur in many other cuisines. Tea can add color and flavor, provide tenderness to meat or poultry, and give a dish that "extra something" to make it intriguing to even the most sophisticated palate, all without fats or sodium.

You can cook with either loose-leaf or tea bag tea but, as always, loose-leaf teas provide more intense flavor and more beautiful color. Although tea liquor left over from a pot you have drunk can certainly be added to a dish, making tea fresh takes but a few minutes and gives a better taste.

The trick is not to heat the water and brew as usual, but instead to let the tea brew naturally in room-temperature water for a longer period of time. As a result, there will be no bitterness even when the tea is heated or cooked in a recipe.

## Make the Most of Those Leftovers

Adding even a tablespoon or two of fresh or leftover brewed black tea (for instance, English and Irish Breakfast, Kenyan, Keemun, or Assam) to gravies and soups adds extra oomph. While it does not overwhelm, it still gives a certain bite and overall more interesting taste.

To brew, place 1 tablespoon black tea leaves in 1 cup spring water; allow to brew for about 20 minutes. Season your gravy to taste by adding a tablespoon of tea to each 2 cups of gravy. Stir ½ to 1 cup tea into a pot of chili, stew, or meat-based soup.

*Tea gives a vibrant flavor to shrimp and rice.*

## cube it!

If you enjoy iced tea, instead of water ice cubes, make tea ice cubes. Simply pour leftover tea into an empty ice cube tray and pop it in the freezer. Next time you are ready to serve iced tea, tap out the tea ice cubes. Not only will they add flavor, but they'll also prevent the iced tea from getting watery.

If you'd rather have a contrasting flavor in your iced tea, make ice cubes from a fruit juice like orange or cranberry juice, or from lemonade — tangy and delicious.

## tea liquor formulas

To make the perfect base for your tea dishes, follow these simple rules.

**Black tea.** Place 2 heaping teaspoons in 1 cup spring water; allow to brew for 20 to 30 minutes. Strain out the leaves and use the tea liquor.

**Oolong tea.** Place 2 level teaspoons in 1 cup spring water; allow to brew for 20 to 30 minutes. Strain out the leaves and use the tea liquor.

**Green tea.** Place 2 level teaspoons in 1 cup spring water; allow to brew for 20 to 30 minutes. Strain out leaves and use the tea liquor.

## CHINESE MARBLED EGGS

Here is one traditional cooking-with-tea recipe that's perfect anytime, for any meal. See the Tea Events menus for other tea-infused recipes in Traditional Eastern Tea Events and Traditional Western Tea Events.

Add the marbled eggs to the menus of the Chinese Dim Sum Tea menu on page 104 or the Chinese Mah-Jongg Tea menu on page 108. These eggs are delicious by themselves, placed atop a salad, or as a garnish. The tea adds both color and flavor to the egg whites.

4 LARGE EGGS
1 CUP BREWED BLACK TEA OF YOUR CHOICE

1. Fill a medium-sized saucepan with water to cover the eggs; cover the pot with a lid. Bring the water to a roiling boil. Turn off the heat and allow the eggs to hard-boil, about 15 minutes. This prevents premature cracking of the shells.

2. Remove the eggs with a slotted spoon. Using the bowl of a teaspoon, gently crack the eggshells all around. Using the slotted spoon, gently return the whole eggs to the original pan of water. Add the black tea leaves, and simmer over low heat for about 20 minutes.

3. Remove the eggs again, and allow them to cool. Shell them carefully. The result will be a "marbled" look on the egg whites. Serve whole or halve them lengthwise, placing the yolk-side down.

*4 servings*

*Don't settle for the usual hard-boiled eggs; perk them up with black tea!*

tea in the
bedroom

*The night has grown old and the moon only half gives us light.*
*The Great Bear is at the horizon, the Smaller already set.*
*This is the evening when I can believe in Spring*
*As insect sounds filter through the warmth of*
*my window silk of green.*
— LIU FAN-P'ING, "A MOONLIGHT NIGHT" (CIRCA 700)

t he bedroom should be geared to rest, relaxation . . . and affection. Lots of families like to gather on king-sized beds to chat, laugh, and do all those little things that bond families together. The bedroom is more than a place in which couples can make love or read a Sunday paper that's spread elaborately all over the bed. It's an important, intimate place to talk quietly about their lives, share their dreams, plan their future.

## Making a Place for "Tea and Ten"

Most bedrooms are not used during the day, making them a perfect tea spot for your personal version of "tea and ten," the absolute minimum 10 minutes for tea you should give yourself every day.

If your bedroom is large enough for a small table, a trunk, or a sturdy ottoman and comfy chair for your tea, it will be easy to dedicate this place as your tea spot. Or perhaps you have a handsome desk and chair to write your most personal correspondence; having a cup of tea while writing dear friends seems to make the words flow easier. Even if your desk is for bill paying, drinking a good cup of your favorite tea can make a dull chore much more pleasant, because you are relaxed and alert from the benefits of the tea. If you're lucky enough to have a window seat, imagine what pleasures you'll derive by making that your own personal place for tea.

There is always enough space to enjoy a cup of tea. At the minimum you can have tea and a biscuit on a tray placed on the bed itself.

# EARL GREY POTPOURRI

This makes a highly aromatic potpourri when placed in a decorative bowl; simply refresh with essential oils every few weeks and it will last for months. The recipe also works well in sachets; put them in your lingerie drawer, or tie them with gorgeous ribbons as party favors to pass out as guests leave. Next time guests visit overnight, place a bowl or sachet of potpourri at the bedside for happy dreams.

Adding an essential oil of bergamot rather than using a ready-made Earl Grey tea provides a vivid scent that is longer lasting in a potpourri. You can use lavender, rose, or orange oil instead of the oil of bergamot. For the tea, choose Nilgiri, Keemun, Ceylon, or English Breakfast. Nilgiri Black teas are particularly good for holding scents.

1. In a large glass, ceramic, or stainless steel bowl, mix together the shredded peels, tea leaves, and dried flowers.

2. Add the oil of bergamot, salt, and balsam of Peru. Stir thoroughly but gently with a wooden spoon.

3. Using a wide-mouth funnel, pour the mixture into glass or ceramic containers. Cork or lid them tightly and store in a cool place for at least two weeks.

**Step 3:** Pour the potpourri into the container of your choice.

**LEVEL OF EXPERTISE:**
easy

**TOOLS AND MATERIALS:**
stainless steel, ceramic, or glass bowl

food scale for measuring ingredients

1 pound grapefruit, lemon, or orange peel, shredded fine

1 ounce loose black tea

8 ounces mixed dried flowers (orange blossoms, petunias, and marigolds)

2 drops bergamot essential oil

1 teaspoon salt

1 ounce powdered balsam of Peru (a fixing agent available at most crafts stores)

wooden spoon

funnel

glass or ceramic containers with tight-fitting lids or corks

LEVEL OF EXPERTISE:
easy, some sewing experi-
ence helpful.

TOOLS AND MATERIALS:
1 recipe Earl Grey Potpourri
(page 53)

scissors

measuring tape or ruler

linen or silk fabric, about 5
inches square for each
sachet

straight pins

sewing needle and thread

liner material of organza,
gauze, or similar mesh
fabric, about 4½ inches
square

ribbon or lace, about 2 feet
per sachet

matching or colorful con-
trasting thread

## EARL GREY SACHETS

This project uses up all those scraps of material that seem to accumulate from other projects. Placed in a dresser drawer, the sachets scent your clothes, accessories, or lingerie for about three months. The potpourri should be aged at least two weeks before using in sachets.

1. Mix together the ingredients of the Earl Grey Potpourri recipe, but you don't need to be so gentle in mixing the ingredients. In fact, slight crushing is important for a more aromatic sachet.

2. Begin with two 5-inch square pieces of silk or linen. Place the squares with right sides facing each other, using the straight pins to keep the edges even. Using the standard size ⅝" or ½" seam, hand sew along three sides with stitches as tiny as you can make them, or make at least two rows of stitches if you can't make them tiny. (This can be done on a sewing machine, if you have one.)

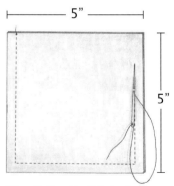

**Step 2:** *Sew the fabric along 3 sides only.*

3. Repeat step 2 with the liner material.

4. Insert the outer material inside the liner and turn inside-out, making sure they fit snugly together.

5. Fill the case with the crushed, aged potpourri to about 1 inch from the top.

6. Turning the raw edges under, sew up the open side of the liner, and then sew up the open side of the outside fabric, overlapping material as necessary.

7. Attach a decorative ribbon or pretty lace around all four edges and across the top to cover up the external stitches and add a nice finish to the project. You could also use the ribbon to make a loop so that the sachet can be hung on an inside closet wall, or on a hanger. Make a bow with the extra ribbon.

**Step 4:** *Insert the outer material into the liner and turn inside-out before filling with potpourri.*

## drying citrus peels

To prepare citrus peels, remove the skins carefully, discarding the white pith. Place the fresh peels on a cookie sheet lined with parchment paper or foil, and heat in a very slow oven, about 150˚F, for about 2 hours. Remove from the oven to cool. When they're cool, shred the peels with a lemon peeler or grater.

About one dozen oranges will make a pound of shredded peels. So, every time you eat an orange, grapefruit, tangerine, or lemon, save its peel. Dry it, and you'll have peels ready whenever you need them for craft projects like these.

## TEA DREAM PILLOW

For sweet dreams, consider the ancient Chinese tradition of using dried tea leaves in silk pillowcases called "dream pillows." At night, put this pillow beside your head or in your pillowcase for a few minutes to help you relax and you'll have the best dreams possible. If you prefer, you can sleep with the dream pillow for the entire night. They make a thoughtful gift for friends; keep a few extras around for houseguests to use while they visit and to take home with them as a token of your hospitality.

LEVEL OF EXPERTISE:
medium; some sewing experience helpful

TOOLS AND MATERIALS:
glass or stainless steel bowl

1 cup dried, unsteeped black tea leaves (such as Keemun or Assam)

2 tablespoons dried lavender flowers

wooden spoon

scissors

½ yard silk

ruler or measuring tape

sewing needle

thread that matches or coordinates with color of fabric

1 yard velvet or lace ribbon (optional)

1. In a glass or stainless steel bowl, thoroughly mix the dried tea leaves and lavender flowers with a wooden spoon.

2. Cut two pieces of silk, each about 9 inches by 7 inches. With the right sides facing each other, sew together along three edges standard ⅝" or ½" seam.

**Step 2:** Sew the silk along 3 edges, leaving one side open.

3. Turn the fabric pocket right-side out. Stuff the tea leaf mixture into the dream pillow, about 1 inch from the edge, and tamp down lightly.

4 Tuck in fabric edges along open side and then sew closed.

5. You can trim the edges by attaching soft velvet or lace ribbon, which not only hides the seams, but also adds a pretty finish to the pillow.

# tea in the bathroom

*Many there are who recite their writings in the bath.*
*How pleasantly the vaulted space echoes the voice!*
— HORACE, *SATIRES*, BK. I., SAT. 4, (35 B.C.)

**W**ant to get away from it all without really going anywhere? Take a soothing bath and don't forget the tea; you can use tea sachets in the water to soften and soothe your skin, or relax with the new commercially available tea-infused face masks, soaps, lotions, shampoos, and shower gels.

Of course, the bathroom is not just for relaxing; it's also for first aid, hygiene, and health care. The following are several modern-day tea-infused formulas that are simple to make, cost pennies compared to over-the-counter or prescription ointments and salves, and — best of all — work.

## BLACK TEA SOOTHER

This is an all-purpose astringent, antibacterial solution for minor cuts, abrasions, and rashes. It is important to *not* use any flavored or scented teas, because the perfumes, oils, or other flavoring agents might be harsh on minor injuries and sensitive skin. Suggested black teas are Keemun, Assam, English or Irish Breakfast, Ceylon, and Kenyan.

½ CUP BLACK UNSCENTED TEA LEAVES
1 QUART BOILING SPRING WATER

1. Brew the tea in the boiling spring water for at least 10 minutes.
2. Strain the leaves and set them aside.
3. Cool the liquid, then refrigerate.

## Uses for Black Tea Soother

This soother is not only for cuts and scrapes; it can be used to soothe irritations or perk up those tired body parts. Always be sure to wipe off any excess solution to avoid staining furniture or clothing.

**Minor cuts and abrasions.** Saturate a pure cotton pad with the Tea Soother and apply to minor cuts or abrasions, allowing it to rest on the laceration at least 5 minutes. Repeat. Do not wash off. This can be done up to four times a day. Repeat the next day, if necessary, but you should see healing by the end of the first day. Keep a small bottle in the refrigerator for minor cuts in the kitchen. Keeps about 10 days.

**Sunburn solution.** Soak a piece of flannel or cotton cloth in the Tea Soother and lay it on the sunburned area. Keep the cloth on until the burned area begins to cool, about 15 minutes. Because tea also has a slight tanning effect, the sunburn may look like a tan but still be a burn. The "tanning" washes off with your next shower or bath. If you remain uncomfortable, repeat this treatment up to four times a day. See your doctor if the skin is still painful by the second day.

**Eye refresher.** Soak cotton pads in Tea Soother; squeeze out the excess and lay them gently on your eyelids. This will help reduce puffiness and soothe red eyes or eyes fatigued from close work such as looking at the computer, reading books, doing needlework, or coin or stamp collecting. Let the pads rest on your lids for about 10 minutes. Repeat if necessary.

Or here's another version of the eye refresher: Instead of making the soother, keep your used black tea bags in the refrigerator and use them on your eyes. Simply lay the cold tea bags on your eyelids and take a 20-minute nap;

*Place used, chilled black tea bags on your eyelids for a quick pick-me-up.*

just the prescription for sparkling eyes. Used tea bags can be refrigerated for up to two days.

**Foot refresher.** Pour a quart of the Tea Soother in a bucket or shallow pan and soak your feet for about 15 minutes. This is excellent for toe fungi, athlete's foot, or minor irritations of the feet caused by running, jogging or standing for long periods at a time. Blot off the excess, but do not rinse the Tea Soother off. Cover your feet with fresh white cotton socks. This is a comforting way to treat your feet at bedtime, but it can be done anytime during the day. Wearing the socks "locks in" the antiseptic quality of the tea.

To help keep your feet healthy, sprinkle crushed dried tea leaves in your socks or shoes. They not only deodorize but also help ward off reinfection of your feet.

## Other Tips for Tea Body Care

Brunettes who have an occasional "moon streak" they'd like to darken can use black tea as a rinse. Brew an unscented, unflavored black tea very strong — about ½ cup tea leaves to 3 cups water — for about 20 minutes. Allow to cool to a comfortable temperature and use as a rinse following your regular shampoo. Do not rinse the tea out. It will make your hair soft and glossy, as well as darker. Rinsing out the tea will rinse off the color, so if you just want to add gloss to your hair, leave on the tea as a conditioner for about 10 minutes and then rinse it out. Style as usual.

What can you do when a tooth hurts and you're nowhere near a dentist? Tea to the rescue. Take a big pinch of spent tea leaves and place directly on the bothersome tooth. Pack the leaves in as much as possible to ease the pain until you can visit the dentist. Replenish as needed, but see your dentist ASAP.

*Choose different types of tea to make different color effects.*

Looking a little peaked? Want to add a touch of Hawaii without taking a trip? You can get a temporary tan by bathing in tea. To brew, use 1 cup unscented, unflavored black tea leaves to 4 cups boiling water. Brew 20 minutes, then cool slightly. Add the strained black tea to a warm bath and soak in it for about 20 minutes. Don't forget your face — saturate a washcloth with the tea water and lay it on your face while you relax in the tub. Your skin will have a slightly browner and rosier hue. Alas, it will wash off during your next shower or bath.

## DYEING WITH TEA

Tea-dyed fabric can be used to make sachet covers, aprons, or anything you'd like to have that "antique" look. Use tea-dyed cloth around the bathroom sink, or as a skirt for a vanity table or chair; cover your walls with tea-dyed cloth rather than paint to make the room quieter, warmer, and more relaxing. Dyeing fabrics with tea is a terrific way to extend the life of worn sheets, or white or beige scrap material. It can give new life to old place mats, doilies, and handkerchiefs.

*Faded old lingerie can be given new life with tea dye.*

Natural materials make the dyeing process easy. And because polyester and polyester blends do not dye evenly, dyeing them with tea will give you interesting variegated patterns, most notably when you intentionally crumple the material during the dyeing process.

For a "textured" look, do not rinse the tea-dyed fabric. Instead, crumple it tightly into a ball, tying it into a knot, and squeezing out as much liquid as possible. Set it aside to dry. For a streaked look, you can hang the wet fabric up to dry over the tub, making the dye run, which will add movement and texture to the pattern. When your fabric is dry, iron flat. If you prefer more of a crinkled look, do not iron. Crinkled fabrics make beautiful wrappings for gifts, and exotic pillow coverings. These methods work for any type of fabric.

LEVEL OF EXPERTISE:
medium

TOOLS AND MATERIALS:
4 cups water

saucepan

10 tea bags of black tea, any
      type or brand

teaspoon

1 tablespoon white vinegar

large tub or bathtub

1 yard white cotton muslin
      (45 inches wide) or one
      ready-made 45-inch-wide
      curtain

old wooden spoon or heavy
      wooden ruler

clock with timer

new rubber gloves

screen or drying rack

## TEA-DYED CURTAINS

Create a softness for the bathroom with tea-dyed curtains for the window. No window? Paint one in the trompe l'oeil style (a realistic scene painted on the wall, floor, or even ceiling of a room) and "cover it" with your tea curtain. The ingredients for dye are easily doubled or tripled, depending on the size of your curtains.

   This project is best done in the bathroom, kitchen, or laundry room — wherever you have easy access to a tub. The container must be large enough for the fabric to float freely; a bathtub is just the right size. If the material is crowded in too small a container, wrinkles will occur.

   If you want to enhance the brown color of the dye, use cider vinegar instead of white vinegar. *Note:* Tea will also dye your spoon and gloves; do not reuse them for anything else.

1. Heat the water in a saucepan to a rolling boil and add the tea bags; turn off the heat. Let the tea bags soak for about 10 minutes and then remove them one at a time with a spoon. As each bag is in the bowl of the teaspoon, wrap the tea tag string around it tightly to squeeze the excess liquid back

**Step 1:** *After soaking the tea bags, wrap the tea tag string around a spoon and squeeze to drain.*

into the saucepan. Repeat until all 10 tea bags are thoroughly drained of the tea liquor. Discard the bags.

2. Add the vinegar to the tea mixture. Pour this mixture into your large tub on top of a table, or pour into the bathtub.

3. Place the curtain fabric in the mixture, stirring it occasionally with the wooden spoon and making sure the fabric is completely saturated with the "dye." For a pale color, 5 minutes should do it. Fabric can be soaked for up to 30 minutes, however; check at 5- and 10-minute increments, remembering that wet fabric looks darker than dry.

4. Wearing rubber gloves, use the wooden spoon to remove the curtain. Squeeze out the excess water.

5. Rinse the dyed curtain with cold running water in the tub until the fabric finally rinses clear.

**Step 3:** *Occasionally stir the fabric in the water for 5-30 minutes, depending on the desired effect.*

6. Dry the fabric flat over a screen or drying rack away from the sun or strong light.

# tea dyeing tips

Here are some tips for creating different dye-effects with tea:

- If you choose a fabric known to shrink in hot water, such as wool or a wool blend, use cool water only for dyeing

- All materials will appear darker wet than dry, so if the color is just what you want, dye it longer to ensure that the shade will still be the one you want when dry

- Tea bags are neater, easy to remove from the "dye," and very economical

- All black and oolong teas will turn fabric some shade of brown, from ecru to beige to brown, depending on how long you soak it. All green teas will make the fabric some shade of green, from pale sage to lettuce to a leafy green. For different hues, use teas blended with fruit or vibrantly colored herbs

# part two
## SHARING TEA WITH OTHERS

*The tea must be chosen for its delicacy and the water for its purity . . . But if even one guest is missing from the assemblage, then the haunting and lasting flavor of the tea must take his place.*
— LU YU, THE CLASSIC OF TEA, ORIGINS & RITUALS (CIRCA 700)

much has been written about the tranquillity of drinking tea as a solo activity not unlike meditation. Yet tea is something that surely must be shared as well. Making the effort, no matter how minimal, of heating the water, putting out lovely drinking vessels, using tea worthy of yourself and your guests, and paying attention to the tea in order to appreciate its gifts of fragrance and taste, are all generous actions. Sharing tea with others is being generous.

One of my favorite Chinese tea legends tells of the goddess of mercy, Kwan Yin. She was embodied as a beautiful statue in a lovely arbor on the outskirts of a small and very poor village. One day a distraught farmer came to the statue and cried for mercy. His village was starving, no work was to be had, no one had any hope. The statue, coming to life for a moment, bent down to touch the farmer's shoulder and give him some direction. "Look," she said, pointing to a small scrap of a plant hidden among weeds and overgrown grass. "If you tend to this plant, watering it, pruning it, taking care of it all the days of your life, it will make you and your village rich beyond measure."

The farmer was so shocked that the goddess had deigned to speak to him that he immediately promised he would do as she suggested, despite his misgivings. Every day, for months on end, the poor farmer came to the plant to water and tend to it, and it grew and grew and grew. Soon there were more plants and *they* grew and grew and grew. Before long the farmer and his village had an entire farm of these plants, tea bushes that gave them a fine beverage to drink and extra leaves to sell. And so they prospered.

In honor of the magnificent goddess, the village created a special oolong process that produced iron black, long, and elegant leaves with a perfume like no other. They named the tea Ti Kwan Yin (Iron Goddess of Mercy). Sharing knowledge about tea, as the goddess did so well, is being kind.

Sharing gifts made for or with the lovely *Camellia sinensis* seems always to bring the giver so much more than he or she ever gives away. This is the essence of the leaf — its ability to connect people, to make anyone who appreciates tea transcend the ordinary. No matter how poor you may be, tea can enrich you.

*Simple canisters of tea can be dressed up with ribbons and lace for gift giving.*

During the Great Depression of the 1930s, when tea bags were used (and reused), tea was always shared. It may be hard to imagine that one tea bag used to make 4 cupfuls could provide delicious tea, but it did. It brought the drinkers comfort as well to share tea with friends and talk of their awesome worries: joblessness, reduced circumstances, and additional mouths to feed. Tea does not find an unemployed person a job, of course, but it can make him feel better about the world for a moment, and that relaxed moment may give him the strength to try again.

Many people got so used to this diluted Depression brew that it took quite a while to recognize and allow themselves the enjoyment of a richly brewed cup of tea. This is not to say that those who drank watered-down tea had no sense of taste, but that sharing tea was always much more important than the brew itself. Tea seems to be the conduit to conversation, the glue of friendship, the link to other cultures, a thread that weaves all the world together.

Wouldn't it be wonderful if all conflicts could be discussed over a cup of tea? Can you imagine world leaders sitting down and making tea for one another rather than being served? What an exchange that would be. This could be done in business as well: The chairman of an auto company could make tea for the president of the labor union, or vice versa. What if, at the beginning and end of a divorce counseling session, husband, wife, and children used a "bowl of tea" as a way to add a touch of softness to otherwise harsh negotiations?

Sharing tea with friends is so easy, so joyful, so enriching. In good times and bad, pausing to talk over a cup of tea makes the happy times more fun, the sad times more endurable. Sharing tea with enemies, real or perceived, may be even more important. Next time a coworker grinds on your nerves, or a customer aggravates, or a family member upsets you, offer a cup of tea. Stopping for even 10 minutes can help you both see what is really important. You never know what you might discover.

# gifts for tea lovers

*. . . that irregular and intimate quality of things*
*made entirely by the human hand . . .*
— WILLA CATHER,
*DEATH COMES FOR THE ARCHBISHOP* (1927)

family traditions handed down from generation to generation are such lovely treasures, but anytime is the right time
to start one of your own. Instead of purchasing birthday
and holiday cards, for instance, why not encourage everyone in your family to make cards? Challenge everyone to
make gifts using their particular skills and talents.

Every parent has a secret stash of those crayon-splashed drawings
and cards made by their children in kindergarten or grade school. When
the children, and the parents, get older, it's even more wonderful to
receive cards and gifts that are made especially for you by the hands
of those you love. The crayons may give way to acrylics, the woven pot
holders turn into hand-loomed place mats or woodworking projects;
perhaps another play with your favorite "stars" singing, dancing, or
acting will be your gift this year.

## HOW TO USE TEA FOR CRAFT PROJECTS

As delicious as your morning tea is, sometimes there is more left over
than you are able to drink. But you needn't throw away the tea liquor
or tea leaves, for they can be used in many different tea crafts. If you
can't work on the project today, refrigerate leftover tea to prevent mold
growth and contamination.

For most projects, choose a breakfast blend, or any black, oolong,
or green tea. Scented or flavored teas should be avoided, because the
natural and synthetic oils added to many teas can turn rancid, and the
scents or flavorings you enjoy while drinking may not be appropriate
in a craft project that needs no fragrance.

If you're not using leftovers, infuse the teas you want to double strength, using twice the amount of tea leaves to the same quantity of water. If it is the leaves themselves you want to use, simply pour on regular tap water to cover them, and infuse until the leaves unfurl enough to be handled easily.

## Using Tea Bag Envelopes and Tea Tags

Tea bags were originally pretty little silk pouches used to sell small quantities of teas to retail customers; they were first used in the early 1900s. Soon, paper gauze was substituted for the silk because it is easy to infuse, an appropriate size for the teacup, and infinitely cheaper.

Though practical and inexpensive, plain tea bags told the consumer nothing about the tea. So in the early part of the century, Sir Thomas Lipton, always on the lookout for ways to promote his product, created the most-copied advertising gimmick of all, the tea tag. Consumers were thus reminded of the manufacturer's name not only when they purchased a box of tea, but also whenever they dunked a tea bag into a cup.

Tea tags have become a charming collectible both as an overview of the progress of advertising art and for the simple beauty of their designs. Tea tags come in all shapes and sizes; some hold only the manufacturer's name, others pithy sayings, and still others artwork that can stand alone as pretty paper ephemera. Generally, tea tags are collected in pairs, so that both front and back can be displayed, and many have a different image on each side. Tea tags from countries outside the United States are quite varied and add to much interest to this hobby.

Following the tea tag phenomenon came the tea bag envelope, which had two purposes: to keep the tea bag fresher longer and, as with the tag, to advertise the tea bag's type of tea and its blender. The many colors and designs used on tea bag envelopes plus their different sizes and shapes, make them excellent paper items for craft projects.

LEVEL OF EXPERTISE:
medium

TOOLS AND MATERIALS:

lightweight self-drying mod-
    eling clay (available at
    arts and crafts supply
    stores)

X-acto knife

premade gift boxes (in any
    shape)

tea sachet envelopes, tea
    tags, or tea-themed gift
    wrap

scissors

paste

acrylic paint

paintbrush

sandpaper

## DECOUPAGE "TEAPOTS"

I love this idea. It's a fun way to use those little gift boxes I keep "just in case" but that only seem to multiply in the closet. It also recycles tea-themed stationery, note-cards, gift wrap, and, of course, tea tags and sachet envelopes.

The object is to create a "teapot" with lid, handle, and spout made of clay, and a bowl made from a box decoupaged with your favorite tea-themed paper scraps. You can make these as large or as small as you like. The smaller ones make good ornaments for decorating large presents or Christmas trees; they can also be hung anywhere they can be viewed to delight you and your guests. I have mine on top of the computer monitor, where they continually amuse me. I have also filled up the larger boxes with sand and used them for paperweights, bookends, and doorstops. Here, function follows form.

1. Make a handle by rolling a quarter-sized piece of modeling clay into the shape of a 3-inch baseball bat, with a narrow bottom and wider top. Then mold it so it looks like a reverse question mark.

**Step 1:** Mold the clay into an oblong shape to make the handle.

2. To create a spout, make another "baseball bat" out of an equal-sized piece of clay. Curve it slightly to resemble a spout then, with an X-acto knife, cut off the narrow end at a slant.

**Step 2:** Make a second oblong shape for the spout, then cut off the narrow end at a slant.

3. Make three balls out of a quarter-sized amount of clay to create a lid and finial. The three balls should be graduated in size from large to small. Flatten both the large and the medium-sized pieces; lay the medium-sized on top of the large. Shape the smallest piece into a triangle and place it on top of the medium-sized piece.)

4. If desired, you can take another quarter-sized piece of modeling clay and divide it into four even balls. Flatten each slightly and use them for "feet" to steady the teapot.

*Step 3: Flatten two balls and top with a triangular piece of clay for the teapot lid.*

5. Cover the small gift box (the body of your teapot) by gluing on tea sachet paper or print paper of your choice.

6. Allow the handle, spout, and lid to dry, then paint them with an acrylic paint that matches or complements the teapot body's paper. Leave them to dry for at least an hour or more, according to the manufacturer's directions.

7. When the paint is dry, attach the parts to the pot with glue. Allow to dry for several minutes, then sand lightly as necessary to make them totally smooth. Touch up as necessary with acrylic paint.

8. Attach a pretty, complementary ribbon to the handle and you have a one-of-a-kind ornament for the holiday tree. Or you can use this on a large present instead of a bow.

*Step 7: Glue the handle, spout, and lid onto the pot.*

LEVEL OF EXPERTISE:
medium

TOOLS AND MATERIALS:

small needlework scissors or manicure scissors

tea bag envelopes

green tissue paper

ruler

pencil

card stock or plain notecards

paste or rubber cement

felt-tip markers with different-sized tips

## GREETING CARDS

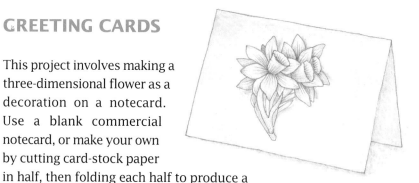

This project involves making a three-dimensional flower as a decoration on a notecard. Use a blank commercial notecard, or make your own by cutting card-stock paper in half, then folding each half to produce a notecard. Select matching envelopes from your stationer or use colored envelopes to coordinate with the decorations you apply to your notecard.

Select a number of tea bag envelopes with a variety of colors. If you want an abstract look, use a number of tea bag envelopes in the same color "family" — pinks, reds, and oranges, for example, or yellows, greens, and blues.

1. Using manicure scissors, cut out the shapes or images from the tea sachets that you like best. Cut out several additional strips of green tissue paper about ¼ inch wide and 3 inches long, along with triangles and circles of your background color from additional tea bag envelopes, or from other paper sources that coordinate with your project.

2. Draw a circle in pencil on the front of the notecard, then pencil in a stem and leaves for your pattern.

3. Filling in your penciled circle to form flower "petals," paste the cut triangles (or other shapes) atop one another in an overlapping manner.

4. Choose a contrasting color of circles and paste them on top of each other to form the "stamen" in the center.

5. Twist together strips of green tissue paper to form the stem, and paste it down.

6. Cut out leaf shapes from additional sachet paper or the green tissue paper and paste them down along each side of the "stem."

7. With a fine-line felt-tip marker of a contrasting color, mark the petals and leaves with lines to accent their shape and give a more three-dimensional effect.

8. Using a broader-nib felt pen, write your sentiment — HAPPY BIRTHDAY, HAPPY ANNIVERSARY, or GET WELL — on the front. Leave the inside blank for a personal message.

**Step 6:** *Cut out leaves or flowers from the envelopes and paste them beside the pencil outline.*

## tea for that special someone

If you have a "special someone" who's crazy about tea, try these suggestions.

- Think tea for two for Valentine's Day or your anniversary. I know of one couple who combine tea and baseball — "outings and innings" — as a way to share their respective passions and spend more time together

- Custom-design a tea basket for anyone you love who's ill or blue; it's a mood lifter and can include food, tea, accessories, books, or your cards handmade with love

- Buy friends gift certificates to the local tea shops with the caveat that they must spend it all on themselves

## Incorporating Tea into Gift Giving

Tea can also inspire gift giving among family members and friends; after all, sharing a tea experience is itself a terrific gift. Here are some more ideas for incorporating tea into your gift giving for people of every age, including yourself.

- Learn ikebana flower arrangements and *chanoyu* tea ceremonies at your local Japanese cultural center, college extension programs, or any of the regional Urasenke centers
- Take a class in ceramics and make your own teapot
- Attend contemporary teapot exhibits at local art galleries
- Sit in on a relaxing *gung fu* ceremony demonstration at regional Ten Ren shops or other fine tea shops in Chinatown
- Attend permanent and traveling shows at your local museums featuring Oriental and/or European porcelain teapots
- Scour flea markets, auction houses, and antiques shops for your favorite tea-related collectibles
- Attend a seminar about tea entrepreneurship
- Take an armchair tour to India, China, Kenya, Japan, or Sri Lanka via a slide show or lecture about the route the *Camellia sinensis* leaf takes from bush to your cup (Or take the real thing by calling your travel agent for a specialty tea tour.)
- Celebrate all the special occasions of your life with a tea party at home or at your favorite tea salon
- Make reservations for Teddy Bear Teas for Christmas at the Ritz-Carlton hotels nationwide; they are as much fun for kids as they are for parents and grandparents
- Take a cooking class at your local kitchenware shop or extension program to learn more recipes for entertaining with tea

# innovative
# tea events

**m**ost Americans associate teatime with the English afternoon tea ceremony, or the Japanese tea ceremony. These celebrations are only two of many ways to incorporate tea in your entertaining, however. Inspirations for tea events are as endless as your imagination.

## AMERICAN PICNIC TEA

*Everything tastes better outdoors.*
— CLAUDIA RODEN, COOKBOOK AUTHOR

Leisurely outdoor picnics have been enjoyed for decades, from a tailgate picnic at the football field to a thermos of tea and motorloaf (a particular type of finger sandwiches) as a respite from the rigors of the English countryside hunt. A picnic can be as sophisticated as a croquet party catered to the max, or it can be something as quick and essential as a break during an invigorating hike.

At home picnics always remind me of the beautifully tree-shaded picnic tables, soft-hammocks, wooden-slatted swing sets, and all the other toys of summer our family enjoyed. Plenty of room to run around and no demands for good table manners were a heady freedom for my cousins, my sister, and me, and we loved picnics to the hilt.

To me, the casual, relaxing mood of a picnic is a quintessentially American form of entertainment. Maybe it's the collective memory of cowboys in the Old West cooking over a campfire, or our own first overnight camp-out with a Scout troop. Maybe it's suburban picnics on the patio with Dad at the Weber, or clambakes on the New England beach with steamed corn and lobsters for everyone. Whatever your preference, make it a top priority to enjoy yourself.

With picnic as a theme, you can introduce a variety of tea-infused foods along with the traditional iced teas for a refreshing, delicious, utterly delightful time. So much preparation can be done in advance that it frees the hosts to truly relax at their own celebration. Even the cooking, usually over the grill, is fun, and done among the guests so everyone can be together, talk, laugh, and be part of this special event.

## Creating Ambience

Casual dining at its best is the mood to set. Bring out the lawn furniture, set up picnic tables and benches or round tables with umbrellas. Add streamers and balloons and you have a colorful, festive setting prepared quickly and with very little expense. Do everything buffet style; the guests can serve themselves in a relaxed manner.

Heat the coals or wood chips prior to the event; this not only speeds up the preparation time for the chef, but also generates that come-hither smell to whet the appetites of the guests.

If your backyard has a pool, consider an aquatic theme with fish motifs; use hot pink, bright yellows, and greens as your colors. One trip to the party store and you'll come away with ideas for a picnic every Sunday.

*A glass of fresh iced tea makes the American Picnic Tea complete.*

## Setting the Table

A trip to a party supply store is for me like a visit to a candy store for other people. I revel in the amazing choices of paper plates, utensils, and cups in so many colors, patterns, and shapes.

Red, white, and blue are the obvious choices for Memorial Day, Fourth of July, or Labor Day picnics. Mini American flags can serve as simple centerpieces. Use tall plastic glasses to hold plastic cutlery; alternate red, white, and blue napkins; and you're set.

(Corn on the cob, coleslaw, and ice cream sundaes are quintessential picnic foods. Recipes for those dishes are not included here, so feel free to use your favorite recipes.)

## LAPSANG SOUCHONG HAMBURGERS

For a variation on this recipe, cook the unbrewed tea leaves directly on the coals or wood in the grill. The leaves will infuse the smoke with their own aroma and taste — ahhhh!

1½ TABLESPOONS LAPSANG SOUCHONG TEA LEAVES
1 CUP SPRING WATER
1 POUND LEAN GROUND BEEF
2 TABLESPOONS BREAD CRUMBS OR MATZOH MEAL
½ ONION, CHOPPED FINE
1 CLOVE GARLIC, MINCED
½ TEASPOON FRESH-CRACKED BLACK PEPPER

1. Brew the tea in cool spring water for about 20 minutes. Strain the leaves, and set aside the liquor.
2. Mix the beef with the bread crumbs, onion, garlic, and black pepper.
3. Form the beef mixture into four patties. Pour tea marinade over the patties and let stand for about 10 minutes.
4. Grill the patties to the desired doneness. Serve alone or on buns with the usual condiments.

*4 servings*

## Baked Potatoes with Green Tea Garnish

4 Idaho baking potatoes

2 tablespoons grapeseed or corn oil

4 pats unsalted butter

1 heaping tablespoon Gyokuro green tea leaves

1. Wash and dry the potatoes, removing any eyes or blemishes. Rub them thoroughly with oil. Wrap each in aluminum foil and grill for 45 minutes or until soft to the touch.
2. Unwrap the potatoes and cut each in half. Scoop out pulp into a bowl and mash with butter. Sprinkle with green tea leaves. Put back into four of the best-shaped potato shells and serve immediately.

*4 servings*

## Green Salad with Mandarin Oranges and Sweet Onions

Canned mandarin oranges are good, too, but offer a sweet taste, versus the tangy citrus taste of fresh. You can amp up the vinegar in your salad dressing to balance the sweet and tart flavors.

2 bunches greens (red or butter lettuce, romaine, or iceberg)

3 mandarin oranges, peeled, pitted, pith removed, segments separated

1 red onion, peeled and sliced very thin (Vidalia or Maui are great too)

Salad dressing of your choice

1. Wash and dry the greens, and tear them into bite-sized pieces.
2. Toss the greens with the oranges and onion.
3. Add salad dressing and toss again; serve immediately.

*4 servings*

## iced tea

A pitcher of icy cold tea is the only drink you need for a picnic or any summertime tea event. It's an ideal thirst quencher with all the picnic foods, savory and sweet. Use ice cubes made of fruit juice to avoid that watery taste most iced teas get when water cubes melt.

Sun tea is truly a superior method for brewing iced tea. Put four bags of tea, such as Nilgiri or Ceylon Black, in a 1-quart glass jar. Pour in spring water to the top and screw the lid on tightly. Set out in a sunny spot the morning of your picnic.

The warmth of the sun is all that's needed to make this good-tasting brew: no bitterness, just good strong flavor, and plenty of it, great for serving over ice. In fact, better set out a few jars. For Independence Day, consider using American Classic Iced Tea, the only tea grown in the United States; it seems a patriotic thing to do.

# RUSSIAN DACHA TEA

*Ecstasy is a glass full of tea and a piece of sugar in the mouth.*
— ALEXANDER PUSHKIN (CIRCA 1830)

In wealthier areas of Russia, from the Czarist era to now, summer homes called dachas have been the setting for meals taken outdoors to capture the short-lived sunny weather. Tea has been an integral part of Russian culture since the Romanovs helped finance many of the five thousand camel loads traveling the Silk Road that brought tea from China to Russia during the 19th century. Each trip took a minimum of 16 months, so I suspect the "aroma" of Russian Caravan tea may have been due more in part to this long trek and the peculiarities of the camels' exertion than any special blending.

Camels, fortunately, are no longer necessary to get tea from China to Russia, because tea comes by air freight, ship, and even train. Today it is the Trans-Siberian Railway that travels through the endless miles of Siberia and other Russian areas, and every passenger seems to have a paper bag of hearty foods and the essential porcelain teapot and cups for constant tea drinking, including that of the blend known as Russian Caravan, which owes its present smoky taste and aroma to Chinese Yunnan and/or Lapsang Souchong.

## Creating Ambience

You don't really need a summer home by the Caspian Sea to have a Russian dacha party. A fancy gazebo or simple shaded table will serve as the buffet area for the food and give guests the feeling of being "away." Unlike most picnics, a refined elegance is the mood here. Set out crisp, lace-edged linens and serviettes, and use your best china and silverware to serve the main entrée. The tea is served hot, and although this seems strange during warm weather, it can be as refreshing on a summer day as an iced tea.

## Setting the Table

Winter or summer in Russia, a towering tea urn, or samovar, is kept heated all day long and through the star-kissed nights, always ready to offer guests or family a glass of hot tea. A samovar, easily rented from any party or catering supply store, will add much to the drama and sophistication of your Russian tea table. They're available in silver plate for a touch of the pretty. Make sure you rent one only used for hot water, never coffee, because the volatile oils from coffee always remain and can contaminate the flavor of your tea.

Fresh flowers from the garden set in an exquisite cut-glass vase, your finest silver or porcelain trays for the food and tea accoutrements, and brilliant white linens will provide a table setting that is luxurious and serenely cool in all white with glints of silver. White flowers would be lovely, or opt for a splash of color.

## STRAWBERRIES RUSSE

This is a very simple, very decadent summer dessert. Direct your guests to help themselves this way: Pick up a strawberry by its leaves, dip into the sour cream, then dip into the sugar. Eat, and drop the leaves into the empty bowl.

2 PINTS FRESH STRAWBERRIES, RINSED, DRIED, STEMS STILL ATTACHED
1 PINT FRESH SOUR CREAM
1 CUP RAW BROWN SUGAR

1. Wash and dry the berries and place them in a large bowl.
2. Put the sour cream in one small bowl and the sugar in another. Set out an empty third bowl.

*4 large servings*

## RUSSIAN BLINIS WITH CAVIAR

1 PACKAGE ACTIVE DRY YEAST (ABOUT 1 TABLESPOON)

1½ CUPS WARM WATER

1½ CUPS ALL PURPOSE FLOUR

1½ CUPS BUCKWHEAT FLOUR

3 LARGE EGGS, SEPARATED

¼ CUP (½ STICK) UNSALTED BUTTER, MELTED

⅛ TEASPOON KOSHER SALT

1 TEASPOON SUGAR

1½ CUPS WARM MILK

   SOUR CREAM

   CAVIAR FOR GARNISH

1. Combine the yeast and warm water in a bowl and set aside in a warm place for about 20 minutes.
2. Gradually add the all-purpose flour and mix thoroughly. Cover with a kitchen towel, and set in a warm place. Let it rise for 1 hour.
3. Combine the buckwheat flour, egg yolks, butter, salt, sugar, and milk in a bowl and add the mixture to the dough, stirring until well blended. Cover, put in a warm place, and allow the batter to rise for about 1 hour.
4. Beat the egg whites in a glass or copper bowl until stiff. Gently fold them into the batter.
5. Drop the batter on a heavily greased griddle by the tablespoon. Cook each blini only until browned on each side. Cool slightly, then place a dollop of sour cream on each. Top the sour cream with caviar.

*about 50 small or 25 large blinis*

# Russian Tea Cookies

This recipe is by Esther Maxwell, grandmother of my friend Amy Ulmer.

2 LARGE EGGS, SEPARATED
1 CUP FINELY CHOPPED WALNUTS
½ CUP SUGAR
1 TEASPOON VANILLA
2 CUPS ALL-PURPOSE FLOUR, SIFTED
1 CAKE (ABOUT ¼ OUNCE) COMPRESSED YEAST
½ CUP (1 STICK) MARGARINE OR BUTTER
½ CUP SOUR CREAM
CONFECTIONER'S SUGAR

1. Preheat the oven to 325° F.
2. Beat the egg whites until stiff.
3. Combine the nuts, sugar, and vanilla. Fold in the egg whites.
4. Put the sifted flour into a large mixing bowl and crumble in the yeast. Cut in the margarine with a pastry blender until the mixture is coarse. Add the egg yolks and sour cream and mix well.
5. Form into a ball. On a lightly floured board, knead the dough until smooth, about 5 to 10 minutes.
6. Divide the dough into three equal parts, wrap each in waxed paper, and chill in the refrigerator for at least 1 hour.
7. On a board sprinkled with confectioner's sugar, roll each dough part into an 8-inch circle. Cut each into eight pie-shaped wedges.
8. Fill the wide end of each wedge with ¾ tablespoon of walnut filling. Roll up from the wide end to the point and place on a greased baking sheet, curving the ends to form crescents.
9. Bake for 25 minutes or until golden. Dust with sugar.

*2 dozen cookies*

## the tea

Like the czars and more affluent Russians did decades ago, you can drink tea Russian style. Select fine sugar cubes or fruit jams. To sweeten your tea, place either a teaspoon of the jam or a sugar cube (or two) directly into the glass. Or take a teaspoon of jam or a sugar cube in your mouth, then sip the tea through the sweetener. If you prefer a more astringent drink, paper-thin slices of lemon would be just fine.

Choices for tea could be a Russian Caravan blend, a smoky Lapsang Souchong, or a rich Chinese Keemun black served in glasses with metal holders for the proverbial "glass-tea" (as my grandmother would call it). If you're unable to find heat-tempered glasses, your prettiest cups and saucers will work equally well.

- Spanish Tapas

- Flan

- Argentina black tea or yerba maté tea (herbal tea)

(Spanish tapas are readily available in most ethic grocery stores, and flan is a popular inclusion in many dessert cookbooks. Recipes for those dishes are not included here.)

## TANGO TEA

How about a fund-raising Tango Tea like those held in the early 1920s at deluxe hotels? You could partake of a sumptuous banquet table of tea foods, drink excellent tea and, perhaps, a gin or two, and with your lover or mate dance that intimate Argentinean-style sensation, the tango. The first hour of the event can be devoted to dance instruction by a tango expert for those "tangled by the tango"; the band can even alternate tango music with traditional ballroom dance tunes to give everyone a chance to dance.

### Creating Ambience

Have a silent auction table of fabulous prizes on one side of the room, and the banquet of food on the other side. Your organization can raise funds with ticket sales that include the dancing instruction, an evening of entertainment, and the food, along with collecting all the money from the silent auction of donations from local merchants.

The silent auction is "silent" because there is no auctioneer. Instead, each item is accompanied by a piece of paper listing its approximate value. Throughout the evening, guests can come by and "bid" by writing down their bid amount and their names. At a specific time in the evening, the band leader or master of ceremonies can call for last bids; those who wrote the highest bid can then claim and pay for their items. The monies go into your organization's coffers to support its cause.

### Setting the Table

Use elegant black and white linens and napery, and set them off with white or red flower centerpieces. Instead of doiles, opt for bright white photocopies of the sheet music of famous tango songs.

Tapas, those savory little bites usually offered at Spanish wine bars, are the perfect foods for your Tango tea. They're hearty, tasty, and easy to eat as finger foods.

## CHAI FOR TWO

Indian culture is rich with romance, from literature to art to cinema. Its wildly popular film industry cranks out movies every week to which audiences go in droves to witness beautiful women flutter their eyes, strong men embrace their beloved to their chests, and all's well that ends with a chaste kiss.

*Make your own chai or purchase one of the many fine commerical brands to serve at your Chai for Two.*

Indian poetry is full of love gained, love lost, love of mortal beings, and love of the Supreme Being. Indian music defies anyone to sit still and not be swayed, lulled, and caressed into a state of relaxation and bliss.

With such a culture of romance, what better tea for a twosome than freshly brewed Masala Chai with delectable flavored scones and sweet Darjeeling-infused peach jam — both from the master tea chef, Robert Wemischner.

### Creating Ambience

Turn on some sitar music or an enchanting Indian singer, and dim the lights or close the blinds. As you drink your tea slowly, feed each other the scrumptious scones. Set out a bowl of cool rose water and a small towel to wash your hands after eating. Turn on the overhead fan to purr redolently above — and there you have it, soft lights, music, a lovers' tea. Now, perhaps you can read a love poem to one another, or perhaps . . .

### Setting the Table

Cover a tray with a pretty place mat and top with contrasting serviettes, two beautiful plates, and two cups and saucers for your tea à deux. On the plates put the scone, a tablespoon of the jam, and a small butter knife. Prepare the tea, decant it into your most exquisite teapot, and place it on the tray.

## CHAI SCONES

The rich, warm spiciness of Masala Chai, a peppery, spicy tea extremely popular in northern India, is fast becoming the "cappuccino of teas" here in America. Chef Robert Wemischner has captured its flavor here in buttery scones. The dough can be made in advance if well wrapped and frozen at 0˚F for up to a month. The recipe uses a premade Masala Chai concentrate (available at most grocery stores).

If made fresh, simply preheat the oven, brush the tops of the scones with an egg glaze, and bake. Let cool until warm, and serve with jam, Devonshire cream, or softly whipped sweetened cream.

4 OUNCES ALL-PURPOSE FLOUR

1 OUNCE WELL-PACKED LIGHT BROWN SUGAR

¼ TEASPOON BAKING POWDER

¼ TEASPOON GROUND CINNAMON

¼ TEASPOON GROUND CARDAMOM

¼ TEASPOON GROUND GINGER

1 OUNCE SWEET BUTTER (UNSALTED)

1 EGG YOLK

2 OUNCES MILK

2 OUNCES MASALA CHAI CONCENTRATE

EGG WASH (1 EGG YOLK MIXED WITH 1 TABLESPOON MILK)

⅛ CUP GRANULATED SUGAR

½ TEASPOON GROUND CINNAMON

1. Preheat the oven to 425˚F.
2. Sift together the flour, brown sugar, baking powder, cinnamon, cardamom, and ginger, and place into bowl of an electric mixer. Add butter. Mix on low speed until the mixture resembles coarse meal.
3. In a small bowl, combine the egg yolk, milk, and Chai concentrate.

4. Add the wet mixture to the dry ingredients in the mixer and mix just until combined; do not overmix.

5. Remove the dough from the bowl to a lightly floured surface and knead briefly. Divide into four small rounds or two large ones.

6. Brush the rounds with the egg wash and score decoratively with a fork, if desired. Mix the granulated sugar and cinnamon. Sprinkle rounds with the cinnamon and sugar mixture, and bake in oven for 15 minutes or until golden brown.

7. Let cool slightly on a rack.

*2 servings*

## MASALA CHAI

If you prefer, you can prepare a homemade chai to use for the scones, and/or to drink along with them. This is my friend Sally Champe's re-creation of flavors she tasted in northern India.

The longer the milk mixture stays refrigerated, the better it gets. To use, stir the mixture and scoop out 2 to 3 tablespoons and add to a cup of very strong, very hot black tea. Then put on a tape of Indian music, relax, and savor the taste of India.

1 6-OUNCE CAN SWEETENED CONDENSED MILK
1½ TEASPOONS GROUND CARDAMOM
¼ TEASPOON GROUND ALLSPICE
¼ TEASPOON GROUND CINNAMON
¼ TEASPOON GROUND CLOVES
⅛ TEASPOON GROUND BLACK PEPPER

Pour the entire can of milk into a clean, dry jar and add all the spices. Cover tightly with a lid, and place in the back of the refrigerator.

*2 servings*

**the tea**

The freshest Darjeeling tea is a must: clean, refreshing, aromatic. Go for the best, like Makaibari's Organic Darjeeling black or exquisitely soft and lighter-tasting silvertips. Other Darjeelings to consider are the Soom Estate and Margaret's Hope. Sikkim's Temi Estate is another exceptional tea to have with this romantic treat. It is best served plain.

This jam is delectable as a sauce for spring rolls, to baste chicken, to top tarts and pies, and to slather all over scones or toast for breakfast. Why not put the extra jam in small jars and give them to friends?

Also created by Chef Wemischner, this jam brings out the fruity character of fine Darjeeling tea. Best of all, it can be made in advance and stored in the refrigerator for at least a month. During the season, use the freshest, ripest peaches redolent with their sweet perfume. Out of season, canned peaches in fruit syrup (no extra sugar added) will do. Defrosted, drained frozen peaches also work well.

16 OUNCES (2 CUPS) SPRING WATER
2 TEASPOONS LOOSE-LEAF DARJEELING TEA
4 POUNDS FRESH PEACHES, PEELED, PITTED, AND ROUGHLY CHOPPED
2 POUNDS GRANULATED SUGAR
½ CUP CHOPPED CRYSTALLIZED GINGER

1. Bring the spring water to 180°F and steep the tea leaves in it for 3 minutes. Drain off the liquor for use in the recipe.
2. Place all the ingredients except the crystallized ginger into a heavy 3-quart saucepan. Bring to a boil over medium heat, skimming frequently during the first few minutes of cooking.
3. Reduce the heat and cook just until the mixture coats the spoon, then flows off slowly. It should have the appearance of a very thin syrup.
4. Add the ginger. Cook for about 15 minutes, stirring frequently.
5. Let stand uncovered at room temperature until cool and then refrigerate, well covered.

*3 quarts jam*

# MOROCCAN TENTED TEA

Here's your chance to be flamboyant and outrageous; to juxtapose richly appointed furnishings with casual. And no need to travel halfway around the world to endure the heat of the desert, the noise and crowds of the bazaars, nor to worry about shipping that bargain of a carpet home. Instead, you can call your local party rental company, rent a white tent, decorate it with some of your own rugs and pillows, and voilà! Morocco comes to you.

## Creating Ambience

Lay carpets (Oriental preferred) on the ground under the tent, several on top of one another; on top of the carpets toss huge, comfy pillows for your guests to relax upon. To the side, have a shallow bowl of warm rose water for guests to rinse their hands, along with some small washcloths or paper towels for guests to wipe their hands dry.

The menu includes flatbreads, which are readily available at ethnic markets and used as "scoops." Please feel comfortable offering your guests forks or spoons to make eating a "neater" experience.

## Setting the Table

Brass is the popular metal of Morocco, and the teapot is tall and graceful with a long, narrow spout. Tea is generally served in glasses with metal handles, and both glasses and teapot are placed on a three-legged brass tray called a *sitya*. Not to worry if you don't have the authentic accessories, though: Your favorite teapot and mugs will do just fine, and any sturdy tray will suffice.

Set a large ottoman or footstool in the center of your tent and place a tray on it to serve the foods. Off to the side, set up a small table covered with fabric; tea and accessories can go here for easy serving. Now relax on soft pillows, tell fanciful stories, and savor Morocco from the convenience of your lawn or patio.

## Savory Couscous

Couscous is a form of pasta and is steamed rather than boiled. It's found in the pasta section of major grocery stores and is ready to serve in about 5 minutes. Follow the directions on the box, or pour boiling water to cover the couscous, cover, and let steam for about 5 minutes. Fluff with a fork. The ingredients you can add to couscous are infinite, and can be anything from savory to sweet. Sweet versions usually include apricots, dates, raisins or currants, and almonds. The following is a savory version, one to remember when you have extra guests some evening and need to extend leftovers.

2 TABLESPOONS GRAPESEED OR OLIVE OIL
1 TEASPOON SALT
4 CUPS WATER
2 CUPS COUSCOUS
½ CUP CHOPPED LAMB
½ CUP SLICED ONIONS
½ CUP LIGHTLY STEAMED FROZEN GREEN PEAS

1. Add the oil and salt to the water and bring to a boil. Add the couscous; stir, cover, and remove from the heat.
2. While the couscous is steaming, sauté the meat and vegetables in a pan until done. Drain.
3. Uncover the couscous and fluff up with a fork. Transfer the couscous to a large bowl and top with the meat and vegetable mixture.
4. Cover to keep warm. Serve immediately.

*4 servings*

## Moroccan Rice Pudding

Serve this pudding in individual ramekins or one large serving bowl. It tastes best when served warm.

1⅓ CUPS WHITE RICE
½ TEASPOON SALT
2⅓ CUPS WATER
¼ CUP (½ STICK) UNSALTED BUTTER
¼ CUP CONFECTIONER'S SUGAR
GROUND CINNAMON FOR ACCENT

1. In a 3-quart saucepan, cook the rice and salt in the water until boiling, stirring only once. Reduce the heat. Cover and simmer for about 15 minutes. Resist lifting the lid or stirring, because it is critical to "steam" this rice for tenderness.
2. Remove from the heat and fluff with a fork. Cover and allow to steam for about 10 minutes more.
3. Stir in the butter and sugar until they are incorporated.
4. Pour into ramekins or a bowl and sprinkle with cinnamon.

*4 large servings*

## inventing your own tea party

The more teas you savor, the more ideas they'll give you for your next gathering — be it a dress-up party at the local retirement home, where everyone dons an outrageous hat and/or boa and has tea and cake; a tea for two with the CD player softly filling the air with romantic music; or the Nonevent Tea Party, where guests are sent invitations, along with excellent-quality tea bags, and a request to stay home, read a good book, sip a cup of tea, and write a check to their favorite charity — especially Friends of the Library.

## Dates & Oranges

½ CUP PITTED DATES

4 LARGE ORANGES, PEELED, SEEDED, AND SLICED INTO ROUNDS

1½ TABLESPOONS ORANGE FLOWER WATER

2 TABLESPOONS CHOPPED ALMONDS

2 SPRIGS FRESH MINT, FOR GARNISH

1. Julienne the dates into four pieces each. Arrange the orange rounds on a serving platter and sprinkle the dates on top of them.
2. Drizzle with flower water. Cover and refrigerate for at least 4 hours.
3. At serving time, lightly toast the almonds in a 250˚F oven for about 10 minutes or until slightly brown. Sprinkle them over the fruit platter and garnish with mint.

*4 large servings*

## Moroccan Mint Tea

This tea is a highly concentrated, very sweet and calming digestive.

2 CUPS WATER

3 TEASPOONS GUNPOWDER TEA LEAVES

15–20 CUBES SUGAR

6 SPRIGS SPEARMINT

1. Boil the water. Place the tea in a pot; pour enough boiling water over the leaves to cover them, then pour that water off.
2. Put sugar cubes on top and fill pot halfway with more boiling water.
3. Lay the spearmint sprigs on top; remove with tongs after a few seconds. Pour into heat-tempered glasses and serve.

*6 servings*

# traditional
# eastern tea
# events

Whether you were raised to enjoy the tea traditions of Canton or London, Tokyo or Bombay, San Francisco or Colombo, all the world's favorite tea ceremonies can be enacted right in your own home. With a little practice, and a few specific accoutrements, you will soon be able to experience, and then share, tea in all its many settings with all your tea-loving companions.

## CHINESE DIM SUM TEA

Sunday afternoon for many Chinese families means dim sum — a time to enjoy those infinitely creative fried or steamed pot stickers and dumplings, savory or sweet. It's enormous fun for a family tea or a casual event for your favorite friends who just want to hang out with you on some weekend afternoon.

Dim sum must be freshly made to be really delicious, but they are really pretty simple to make. Following you will find several selections to stimulate your interest and curiosity. You do have three choices, however: Make your own, purchase frozen selections, or get takeout from a Chinese restaurant. (I won't tell.)

### Creating Ambience

Laughter, lively conversation, all the friendly noise of family teatime are part of the Chinese dim sum party; this is not an occasion for quiet reserve, so thoroughly enjoy yourself.

No special decorations are required; all that's really needed are you, your family, and your friends.

## Setting the Table

A lazy Susan is a fixture at many Chinese restaurants, and with good reason: It makes serving a group like a family or a horde of friends easy for the host and the guests alike. Set the table with a dessert-sized plate for each person, a small handleless cup for the tea, and chopsticks.

Because several of the dishes are finger foods and can be slightly messy, place a hot, damp washcloth on a porcelain plate beside each guest. Set out tiny plates for condiments such as rice vinegar, chili sauce, soy sauce, or mustard, depending on the dim sum you choose. Serving plates or baskets should be placed around the table or on the lazy Susan, with a pot of tea for every four people. Restaurant dim sum are usually served in steamer baskets or on plates with three to four pieces each; you can do the same, or just use covered bowls or plates. This menu is geared for four people for tea or light supper for two.

*While you don't need a Chinese teapot to enjoy the Dim Sum Tea, this vessel will add to the ambience.*

 CHILLED LYCHEE

Lychee are pale pink fruit that offer a delicate, perfumed sweetness. Served chilled, lychee cleanse the palate, balance the yin-yang of a Chinese meal, and offer a refreshing finale to the spiciness of the recipes on this dim sum menu. You can find cans of lychee in the Oriental section of any major supermarket.

1 8-OUNCE CAN LYCHEE

1. Open the can at least 2 hours prior to serving time, and chill the lychee in a large bowl covered tightly with plastic wrap. At the same time, refrigerate four small dessert bowls.
2. At the end of the dim sum service, pour the chilled fruit and some of its syrup into the chilled bowls. Serve with a dessert spoon.

*4 servings*

(Opt for frozen or restaurant takeout pot stickers if you don't want to make that part of the meal. Recipe for this dish is not included here.)

## Chinese BBQ Chicken Wings

These are deliciously messy, so offer each guest cloths soaked in hot water for cleanup.

4 TABLESPOONS KETCHUP
2 TABLESPOONS HONEY
1 TABLESPOON WHITE VINEGAR
1 TABLESPOON SOY SAUCE
¼ TEASPOON SALT
2 CLOVES GARLIC, CRUSHED
1 POUND CHICKEN WINGS, TIPS REMOVED

1. In a bowl, combine the ketchup, honey, vinegar, and soy sauce. Add the salt and garlic, and mix well.
2. Rinse and wipe dry the chicken wings. Place them in the bowl of marinade and toss, covering them thoroughly.
3. With tongs, pick up the wings and place them on a foil-lined cookie sheet. Bake at 350°F for about 30 minutes, turning once.
4. Remove from the oven and arrange on a platter.

*4 large servings*

## Hot Shrimp on a Stick

Skewers aren't common in Chinese cooking, but they make a neater presentation. If you don't have any, arrange the shrimp gracefully on small plates with a mound of grated carrots in one corner of each plate.

48 SMALL OR 24 LARGE SHRIMP, PEELED AND DEVEINED
1 TABLESPOON PEANUT OIL
1 TABLESPOON CHINESE FIVE-SPICE POWDER

1 TABLESPOON SOY SAUCE
3 TABLESPOONS WATER
FRESHLY GRATED CARROTS FOR GARNISH

1. Place raw, deveined shrimp on skewers and lightly brush them with the peanut oil.
2. In a small bowl, mix the seasoning, soy sauce, and water, and whisk thoroughly.
3. Coat the shrimp evenly with the sauce. Grill or broil for about 2 minutes on each side for smaller shrimp; 3 to 4 minutes for prawns.
4. Serve on small plates with a garnish of fresh-grated carrots.

*4 servings*

## GARLIC CHINESE LONG BEANS

Traditional or Blue Lake green beans can be substituted for Chinese long beans; buy beans that are not too thick. Whichever you use, cut the beans into 4-inch pieces so that they're easy to handle.

1 POUND FRESH CHINESE LONG BEANS (ABOUT 12 TO 18 INCHES LONG)
4 CLOVES GARLIC, SLICED
1 TEASPOON PEELED AND MINCED FRESH GINGER
1 TABLESPOON PEANUT OIL (CANOLA OR SAFFLOWER OIL CAN BE USED)
4 TABLESPOONS SOY SAUCE

1. Steam the green beans just until crisp, then drain them and keep in a warm bowl.
2. Sauté the garlic and ginger in oil until slightly brown; do not burn. Remove from the heat; add the soy sauce and mix thoroughly.
3. Pour garlic mixture over beans and toss well. Serve immediately.

*4 large servings*

The typical accompaniment for Chinese dim sum is an oolong or jasmine tea, but my suggestion is to try a black tea such as Keemun or Yunnan. Or try a pu-erh, a hearty tea that is a superb aid in digesting rich foods. These teas provide the right balance of flavor and soothing quality to rich dim sum. Loose leaves, as always, provide more taste than tea bags, but use what is readily available to you.

## CHINESE MAH-JONGG TEA

The fast-paced tile game called mah-jongg is just the right entertainment for a dim sum party, especially for those who would rather eschew the quiet concentration of the chess board or bridge table for a considerably more social game. Not that mah-jongg isn't serious; many people bet on the outcome of their playing, and winnings can be considerable, but most groups spend their collective winnings on trips to the theater, concerts, or even mini vacations rather than pocketing it all themselves. This way, they extend the pleasure of the game, and certainly extend the social fun of being with one another.

### Creating Ambience

A corner in the living room with a card table and four chairs is really all you need to play mah-jongg. Because a table of this size is limited, just keep a teapot and cups for tea handy during the game. For serious eating of your Mah-Jongg Tea meal, serve the food buffet style, allowing your guests to help themselves. If you'd rather serve more formally, then by all means set up everything on the dining table.

### Setting the Table

If you have a second set of mah-jongg tiles, you can stack them into different fanciful shapes or simply scatter them around the table. The colors typically found on tiles are red, green, blue, and yellow, and the tile background is usually an ivory color. Select paper plates and napkins to match or contrast; you could even gather flowers in those colors to place on the table.

Put out hot washcloths on plates or bamboo holders, along with both chopsticks and forks so that your guests can choose what they'd like to use.

*Mah-jongg, the popular Chinese tile game, is an*
*excellent accompaniment to dinner with friends.*

# TOFU CILANTRO

This is another example of how a dish can be simple, with just a few ingredients, yet taste divine. Use black or dark green plates to show off the whiteness of the tofu.

1 POUND FIRM TOFU

1 TABLESPOON CANOLA OIL

6 GREEN ONIONS, BOTH GREEN AND WHITE PARTS, SLICED

3 TABLESPOONS SOY SAUCE

3 SPRIGS CHOPPED CILANTRO (AKA CHINESE PARSLEY)

1. Drain the tofu in a bowl by placing a heavy plate on top of the bean cake. Let stand for about 10 minutes. Pat dry with paper towels, then cut into 1-inch thick slices. Arrange two slices each on four small plates.
2. Heat the oil in a skillet until hot, then stir-fry the green onions over medium heat for about 3 minutes, or until crisp. Remove the pan from the heat, pour the soy sauce over the green onions, and stir, scraping the pan for any crusty pieces.
3. Slowly pour the mixture over the bean curd and sprinkle with the chopped cilantro. Serve immediately.

*4 servings*

## mah-jongg
## tea menu

- Tofu Cilantro

- Paper-Wrapped Chicken

- Steamed Chinese or
  Italian Broccoli

- Sliced Melon Mélange

- Chinese Jasmine or
  Ti Kwan Yin oolong tea

## PAPER-WRAPPED CHICKEN

In mainland China cooks use edible paper for this appetizer. Only some smaller Chinatown shops in the United States carry such paper, though. Instead, you can use baker's parchment paper or aluminum foil.

1 WHOLE CHICKEN BREAST, DEBONED, SKIN REMOVED

1 TABLESPOON SOY SAUCE

1 TEASPOON DRY SHERRY

1 TEASPOON OYSTER SAUCE

½ TEASPOON SUGAR

1 TEASPOON ARROWROOT

¼ TEASPOON SALT (OPTIONAL)

¼ TEASPOON SESAME OIL

PARCHMENT PAPER, WAXED PAPER, OR ALUMINUM FOIL (ABOUT 1 FOOT)

1. Cut the chicken breast into 1-inch squares and flatten with mallet or heavy knife.
2. Combine other ingredients in a bowl and mix well. Add chicken pieces and marinate in the refrigerator for at least 30 minutes.
3. Cut the parchment paper, waxed paper, or aluminum foil into 20 4-inch squares. Arrange the squares before you like diamonds. Place a chicken piece just below the center of each square, fold the bottom point up over the chicken, and fold in both the sides. Tuck the top point inside to "close" the packet.
4. Deep-fry the paper packets four at a time in a wok heated to 375°F for about 3 minutes. Drain and place on a heated platter. If you're using foil, bake the packets on a cookie sheet for 30 minutes in a 350°F oven.

*4 servings*

## Steamed Chinese Broccoli

Chinese broccoli is thinner and longer than Italian broccoli but has a similar taste. The Chinese version is available nearly year-round at any Asian market, but Italian broccoli is easily substituted. Serve with a drizzle of fresh lemon juice and a sprinkle of zest. Nothing more!

1 POUND CHINESE BROCCOLI
FRESH LEMON JUICE FOR TOPPING
LEMON ZEST FOR GARNISH

Steam the broccoli for about 6 minutes or until brilliant green and tender enough for a fork to pierce the stalks. Serve with lemon juice and lemon zest.

*4 large servings*

*Chopsticks aren't a necessity for the Mah-Jongg Tea, but add that extra Asian flavor to the event.*

### the tea

For this party, consider serving two different teas: a hearty, pungent Ti Kwan Yin oolong with the meal, and a light, delicate jasmine or Lu'an Melon tea with the dessert. The group can play a full game of mah-jongg between the entrée and the dessert, thus allowing the hostess time to clear the dishes and prepare a pot for the second type of tea and serve the dessert.

# SLICED MELON MÉLANGE

Summertime is the best time for melons, and the variety is growing each year, from Casaba to Persian to the commonly available honeydew and cantaloupe. Pick the ripest, most aromatic melons, and use about half a melon per person.

Serve in clear glass bowls to show off the pretty pastel colors of the melon. Spoons are better than forks to scoop up every fragrant drop of juice. If you prefer, use a melon baller to form pretty balls of the melon pulp, or mix and match with slices and balls.

3 DIFFERENT TYPES OF MELON (E.G., CASABA, HONEYDEW, CANTALOUPE, WATERMELON)

Seed, slice, and peel the melons. Mix the melon slices together in a bowl; do not refrigerate, because melons are sweeter and more delicate at room temperature. Serve a mixture of melon types in individual bowls.

*6 servings*

*Simple, beautiful, and delicious, a dessert of sliced melons is sure to be appreciated by guests.*

## JAPANESE TEA

Learning *chanoyu,* the formal Japanese tea ceremony, is a lifelong process, a spiritual journey that is a welcome mini retreat from the hustle-bustle of everyday life. You can, however, translate the essence of the ceremony into a simple Japanese Tea at home. You needn't buy or use Japanese accessories, but they're so interesting and relatively inexpensive that they can only add to your enjoyment and that of your guests.

### Creating Ambience

Quiet, uncluttered, and serene are the feelings a Japanese setting should evoke. You could create a setting within a setting by opting to use your living room or den. Move enough of the furniture away so that you can walk around the coffee table. Set pillows on the floor around the table. If you have a folding screen, it would be the easiest way to "shut out" the rest of the room and the "ordinary world." The objective is to create a feeling of harmony and stillness.

Listen. Are there sounds you can muffle or eliminate by closing doors or shutting windows? Flutists James Galway and Jean-Pierre Rampal have both recorded exquisite Japanese music to create a soft background for your tea; however, silence and gentle conversation are all you really need to create the serenity of a Japanese tea meal.

On a covered box or sturdy footstool, place a vase with one perfect flower, or top it with a piece of artwork you love: something simple and perfect.

### Setting the Table

Set the table with crisp linens as place mats and serviettes. Add plates, chopsticks, teacups, and teapots. Japanese-style cups and plates are generally different shapes and sizes with similar, but not identical, hues and patterns; they're made of good clay. It is not nec-

(Because miso soup is easy to find in the specialty section of most supermarkets, the recipe is not included here.)

essary to have these serving pieces; use those plates and cups that are most appealing to you. Those in soft, comforting colors or interesting shapes, such as hexagonal, square, or rectangular, add interest to the table.

## Brewing and Serving the Tea

Now you are ready to serve your tea. Consider a sencha or genmaicha, both readily available at any tea shop or Japanese food shop, and the Asian sections of many major supermarkets.

To make green tea, boil the water and swirl a little in your teapot to warm it up. Allow the boiled water to cool to 170 to 185°F. Empty the water from the teapot and put a teaspoon of green tea leaves in your warmed pot for every 6 ounces of water; fill the pot with hot water, and allow to steep for only a minute. Taste. Let steep longer, if desired. Pour all the tea off the leaves into the cups. If you have leftover tea, pour into a warmed creamer to serve your guests refills.

In Japan it is considered customary to make a slight slurping noise when you drink tea. Always pick up the cup with your right hand and support the cup on your left hand, and sip while using both hands to hold the cup; practicing just a few times will enable you to do this gracefully.

*The traditional Japanese iron teapot looks stunning on its own.*

## Miso Soup

Miso soup comes in packets found on the Asian food shelves of super-markets. Simply add hot water, stir, and pour into covered bowls. It is customary to sip soups rather than use a spoon, but chopsticks can help diners eat miso's tofu and sweet green seaweed.

## Mock Sushi Rolls

Sushi may be eaten with fingers or chopsticks. Fortunately, ready-made sushi is now available at major supermarkets and Japanese restaurants.

English cucumbers are crisper and sweeter than "regular" cucumbers, which need to be salted and drained of their bitter water.

½ English or hothouse cucumber

3 tablespoons seasoned rice vinegar

½ teaspoon sugar, if rice vinegar is unseasoned

¼ pound thinly sliced prosciutto ham

Cilantro for garnish

1. Peel the cucumber and cut into 2-inch pieces; seed and then julienne. Place in a bowl and sprinkle lightly with rice vinegar and a dash of sugar (if rice vinegar is unseasoned). Drain and pat dry.
2. Lay out a slice of the ham on a cutting board, place the julienned cucumbers atop it horizontally, and roll them up tightly in the ham. Slice the rolls into 1-inch rounds, and arrange three each on individual dishes.
3. Garnish with cilantro and a small portion of hearty mustard or the spicy-hot Japanese horseradish, wasabi.

*about 6 servings*

A rice cooker makes this a snap, but if you don't have one, you can certainly cook the rice on the stove as instructed below. This is a good recipe for those new to sushi, because the shrimp are cooked.

4 LARGE PRAWNS (SHRIMP)
BOILING WATER TO COVER
1 CUP SHORT-GRAIN RICE
1 CUP WATER
SUSHI VINEGAR
1 TABLESPOON PREPARED WASABI, OR TO TASTE
2 MEDIUM PIECES LETTUCE, WASHED AND DRIED (DECORATION ONLY)
2 TABLESPOONS PICKLED GINGER
2 SLICES LEMON, HALVED

1. Bring enough water to cover the shrimp to a boil. As the water is heating, wash the shrimp thoroughly and devein with a toothpick inserted between the joints and the shell. Remove heads.
2. Starting at the top of each shrimp, put a bamboo skewer through it (to keep it straight). Drop them into boiling water. As soon as they rise to surface, take them out and put into a bowl of ice water.
3. Peel off the legs and shell of each shrimp but leave the very tip of the tail intact. Turn the shrimp over and butterfly it by slicing along the center of the bottom, then turning the shrimp inside out. Refrigerate, covered, until serving time; preferably within hours.
4. Bring rice and 1 cup water to a boil over medium heat, then cover tightly and boil over high for 2 more minutes. Reduce the flame to medium again for 5 minutes, then reduce to low for 15 minutes.
5. Remove pan from the heat. Remove lid, drape a linen cloth over the top of the pan to absorb steam, and let cool for about 15 minutes.

6. Put rice into a nonmetallic container and, with a flat wooden paddle spoon, spread it evenly. Then plow through rice in a left-to-right, top-to-bottom motion repeatedly again until grains are separated.

7. Add enough sushi vinegar to stick the rice together without turning it mushy, about ⅓ cup or more. Using a piece of cardboard, fan the rice to cool it as you continue to plow through the rice.

8. To serve, form sushi rice into a rectangular shape matching the body of the shrimp. Dab a little wasabi on rice, and place shrimp on top. Place two shrimp on a piece of lettuce on a pretty plate. Garnish with a small mound of pickled ginger and thin slices of lemon.

*2 servings*

## GRILLED CHICKEN

2 TABLESPOONS SOY SAUCE
½ TEASPOON MINCED GARLIC
½ TEASPOON MINCED AND PEELED FRESH GINGER
2 CHICKEN BREASTS, DEBONED, WITH SKIN ON
THIN-SLICED LEMON, FOR GARNISH (OPTIONAL)
THIN-SLICED STRIPS OF HOTHOUSE CUCUMBER, FOR GARNISH (OPTIONAL)

1. Mix the soy sauce, garlic, and ginger. Marinate the chicken breasts in the mixture, refrigerated, for about 20 minutes.

2. Drain the chicken breasts and broil or sauté them for about 4 minutes on each side, until done.

3. Remove the chicken from the pan and slice it diagonally into ¾-inch strips. Position them at an angle on a rectangular or square plate; garnish the corners of the plate with thin-sliced lemon and thin strips of English or hothouse cucumber rolled into an upside-down "cone." Other vegetable garnishes are equally good.

*2 servings*

## other dessert options

Quarters of pears or apples, seeded and sliced partway through at one end to look like wings; melon balls in pretty bowls; or a traditional cup of mixed fruit — all would be lovely finishes to this Japanese Tea meal.

You can serve each cup on a pretty coaster. Add a decorated toothpick with which guests can pick up pieces of the orange to eat.

1 SWEET ORANGE

Trim off the base and top of the orange so it can be balanced on a plate. Using a very sharp paring knife, cut the orange in a zigzag all around the center, making sure to cut right through the pulp. Carefully open the two halves of the orange. Cut all around the inner pith and slice through the wedges of the oranges.

*2 servings*

# traditional western tea events

everyone in the United States, except our Native Americans, is a descendant of someone who came from somewhere else. Immigrants from Europe during the eighteenth and nineteenth centuries, in particular, brought many tea traditions that reflect their original cultures: the British brought their love of hearty blacks, served with milk and biscuits; the Russians brought their samovars, glasses with silver or brass holders, and jams and lemons for flavoring tea; the French brought their many-flavored tea favorites and delectable pastries.

The revolution of 1776, of course, greatly interrupted the pleasures of tea for many years, and some of the most patriotic Americans still drink coffee over tea simply for reasons of politics rather than palate preferences.

In the late 19th century, thousands of Chinese came to build our railways and mine our gold, bringing with them the oldest of tea traditions. Since then, the Japanese, Koreans, and other pan-Asian cultures have followed, each bringing tea traditions to their new home. What results is the traditional melting pot element of our culture. We can drink a Chinese Dragonwell in a celadon Korean bowl placed on an exquisite Japanese black lacquer plate, set it upon our grandmother's Welsh oak table while eating French pastries with Danish silver and telling African folktales or singing songs from popular composers of every ethnic background.

Perhaps the only intrinsically American tea tradition is iced tea, a marvel of both refreshment and marketing savvy that began during the world's fair of 1904, held in the scorching heat of St. Louis, Missouri. Unable to sell his hot tea, entrepreneur Tom Sullivan plopped a few ice cubes into a glass and offered it to a few customers, and today eighty percent of all tea drunk in the United States is iced tea.

Entrepreneurs of the '90s are as creative, producing iced tea lattes, chilled masala chais, and traditional iced teas flavored with the most exotic fruit and flavorings possible. If it's cold, flavorful, and in a tall glass, American iced tea drinks will remain popular forever.

## ENGLISH AFTERNOON TEA

Perhaps no tea celebration is better known than that convention of both the Victorian and the Edwardian eras, the afternoon tea. Ironically, this tea is rarely served with much elaboration in England anymore, but is hugely popular in the United States and increasingly popular in Japan.

The tradition allegedly began in 1840 when Anna, the seventh duchess of Bedford, felt a "sinking feeling" one afternoon between gown fittings, shopping, and preparing for a long and elaborate dinner. Her lady in waiting, to whom we all owe gratitude, fetched a cup of tea and some toast for her mistress, and Anna felt much better.

In fact she liked this idea so much that she soon invited some girl-friends over to the royal quarters to gossip a bit and sip a cup or two. But as hostesses are wont to do, she thought her guests were entitled to something a little more special than toast and tea. So added were a cake or two and some little sweets — and a tradition was born.

Throughout Queen Victoria's lengthy reign, the tea became ritualized, formalized, and socialized to the point that ladies and gentlemen called upon friends at their homes, calling cards in hands, to sit for a pleasant hour or two, discuss the literature, art, and music of the day, and share in a gossipy exchange. (Some things can't change.)

Afternoon tea is sometimes referred to as low tea, because it is served in a parlor or living room at a low table, usually a portable butler's tray that rests firmly upon a quartet of sturdy legs. On this a pot of tea is placed, to be served either plain or with milk — never cream — along with the traditional scones or crumpets, finger-sized sandwiches, and dainty, bite-sized desserts or perhaps slices from a rich and delicious cake.

This charming repast is *not* a high tea, no matter how "high society" the tea experience may sound. The event is *afternoon tea*. High tea, which involves a meat dish served at a high table, is completely different. For more on high tea, see the Monday-Night Football High Tea on page 124.

## Creating Ambience

The whole point of afternoon tea is to offer your guests comfortable seating, match up guests who can talk engagingly, and enjoy your well-prepared tea with foods as decorative as they are tasty.

Because the menu of an afternoon tea is primarily made up of finger foods, large cloth serviettes (napkins) are important. Gracefully placed on the lap, serviettes catch the errant crumb, save your upholstery or carpet from stains, and offer a soft tactile experience when you wipe your fingers.

End tables, sturdy wooden TV tables, or the aforementioned butler's trays are critical for afternoon tea served in a living room. You can not gracefully drink tea, butter your scone, and bite into a petit four all at once. So providing reliable surfaces on which guests can place plates or cups and saucers is important. (Serving tea in the dining room certainly is easier for both the guests and the host, but dining chairs are not always as comfy as a plump sofa with downy pillows.)

You don't need to be an Anglophile to enjoy the coziness of a fire in the winter or the cool breeze on the porch in the summer, but if your home has neither, do not despair. A clean, softly lit room, well-placed furnishings, and easy access to the food and tea are all gracious reflections of your warmth and consideration for your guests. And that is always what hospitality and tea are about.

## Setting the Table

Porcelain teapots and china cups, china plates, and linen or cotton serviettes are all typical elements of an afternoon tea table setting, but nothing need match. Just as mixing chintz with lace is perfectly acceptable English decor, so is mixing pretty pink depression glass with rose-covered platters and an occasional majolica dish.

One idea to keep in mind when putting out tea foods on a buffet is to make the eye "move" by using serving pieces of various heights — for instance, place cake stands or other pedestal platters next to flat silver trays or bowls. In the middle put a vase of flowers, underneath it lace over colored napery, and you have a feast for the eye as well as the stomach.

Place cards are traditionally used to identify guests, but they are also a pretty touch when placed on the buffet to identify the dishes you are serving. These are a cinch to make and add a touch of whimsy to the buffet table.

*A simple, elegant teacup with an antique silver infuser are set on fine linens.*

LEVEL OF EXPERTISE:
easy

TOOLS AND MATERIALS:
store-bought place cards

pencil

paste or rubber cement in a
container with a very
narrow spout

tea fannings (the powder of
crushed tea leaves) or tea
bag tea

large piece of plain paper or
newspaper (to work on)

# TEA LEAF PLACE CARDS

These place cards, lettered with actual tea leaves, will add a unique accent to your next tea, whether to identify your guests or various tea table treats. If you prefer to make your own, simply buy 8½-inch by 11-inch card stock, cut to the size you want, and fold each piece in half horizontally so it can stand on its own. One sheet can make four place cards 4¼ inches wide and 2¾ inches deep. Folded in half it will be 4¼ inches wide and 1⅜ inches deep.

The vivid chartreuse of *matcha,* the ground tea of the Japanese tea ceremony, is a pretty alternative to the brown or black tea, although gilt paint can be applied for a richer look. Allow the glued tea to dry for at least 20 minutes, then paint with the gilt, using a fine-point brush to add accents and flourishes to the letters.

1. On the front of each card, lightly pencil in the food item or person's name as desired. If you're an excellent calligrapher, you can do this in ink, but use a very fine-line nib for your pen.

2. Squeeze a very thin line of glue along the penciled or inked writing. Scoop up a teaspoon of the ground tea leaves and follow the outline of the glued areas. Repeat, to ensure that all glued areas are covered.

**Step 2:** *After adding a thin line of glue to the outlines, sprinkle ground tea leaves on top.*

3. Gently turn the place card over above a large sheet of paper, and lightly tap it to shake off loose tea. Allow to dry completely.

## MENU PLACE CARDS

Choose paper, pens, and tea tags to coordinate with the other colors used in your table setting. For example, if you're using a colorful tablecloth, use white or beige card stock. Or if all your napery is white, use a card stock to match either your teacup patterns or the plates you use. Be sure to write on both sides of the card, and place the card to the right of each dish. This way, whether your guests are on one side of the table or the other, they'll be able to see the card and identify the dish.

Instead of tea tags, you might also use your favorite stickers, images cut out from tea bag sachet envelopes, or paper scraps you've cut out from magazines. The place cards certainly don't have to all be the same.

1. Cut out 3-inch by 6-inch pieces of cardstock and fold in half horizontally.

2. Remove each tea tag carefully from its string. At the top midpoint of each place card, paste a tea tag on each side so that the most artful image is showing.

**Step 1:** *Cut out and then fold in half several pieces of 3" x 6" cardstock.*

3. Using a colored pen, write in the name of the dish on both sides of the card.

LEVEL OF EXPERTISE:
easy

TOOLS AND MATERIALS:
scissors

ruler

sheets of card stock

tea tags, 2 per place card

glue or paste

colorful calligraphy pens

## TEA TALK SCONES

For more than a decade, I have served these scones with lemon curd. The recipes originally appeared in the first year of publication of my newsletter, *TEA TALK, a newsletter on the pleasures of tea.*

Scones should be served warm. After removing them from the oven, place them in a linen or cotton cloth and put the cloth in a basket for serving. Suggested accompaniments include butter, clotted or whipped cream, jams or preserves, and, of course, Tea Talk Lemon Curd.

Dried cranberries, currants, golden raisins or sultanas, or other dried berries work well instead of the raisins.

2 CUPS WHITE FLOUR

4 TABLESPOONS SUGAR

1 TEASPOON CREAM OF TARTAR

1 TEASPOON BAKING SODA

½ TEASPOON SALT

½ CUP UNSALTED (1 STICK) BUTTER OR MARGARINE (STICK ONLY; DO NOT USE SOFT OR WHIPPED)

¾ CUP MILK

¾ CUP RAISINS

1. Preheat the oven to 400°F.
2. Sift together all the dry ingredients and cut in the butter until you have a coarse mixture. Add milk to make a soft dough, then add the raisins and mix well.
3. Roll out the dough to ½ inch thick. Use a 2-inch cookie cutter to carve out scones or, if you prefer, drop heaping tablespoons of dough onto an ungreased cookie sheet.
4. Bake for about 12 to 15 minutes, or until golden brown.

*About 10 large scones*

## Tea Talk Lemon Curd

The curd keeps well in the refrigerator, usually for up to a month, but it usually gets eaten up before any typical "expiration date" could be applied. I save small jars during the year for containers of curd, my traditional holiday gift.

Use Tea Talk Lemon Curd directly on scones like a jam, or use as a filling for mini tarts.

2 LARGE EGGS PLUS 2 LARGE EGG YOLKS
¾ CUP SUGAR
⅔ CUP FRESHLY SQUEEZED LEMON JUICE (ABOUT 3 LEMONS)
2 TEASPOONS GRATED LEMON PEEL
⅓ CUP (⅔ STICK) UNSALTED BUTTER, CHILLED AND CUT INTO SMALL PIECES

1. In a heavy-bottomed 1½-quart saucepan, whisk the eggs and yolks together. Add the sugar, juice, and lemon peel. Sprinkle in a few grains of salt and add the butter pieces.
2. Cook the mixture over low heat, stirring constantly with a wooden spoon (metal sometimes reacts with the lemon). Cook until it thickens enough to coat the back of the spoon, about 8 minutes. *Do not let mixture boil,* or the yolks will curdle.
3. Pour the mixture into a heat-proof glass dish and cover with plastic wrap. Refrigerate for at least 4 hours before serving. Refrigerate unused portions.

*1 ½ cups*

**the tea**

Darjeeling is the champagne of teas, a lively, brisk tea for afternoon. The finest are best plain, but Darjeeling can be served with a drop of milk. Other choices might be a fruity black Cameroon or a floral tea from the Temi Estate in Sikkim.

## the origin of the sandwich

We have John Montague to thank for the development of what is now called the sandwich. In 1762, famished after exhaustively working at his desk on duties for his dual posts as Great Britain's Secretary of State and First Sea Lord, he asked his valet to just bring two slices of bread and a slab of beef. He put them together to eat out of one hand while he continued to work with the other.

Montague, whose title was the fourth earl of Sandwich, often worked at his desk for 12 hours at a time. The legend that he requested the "sandwich" so as not to disturb a winning streak at the gaming tables has been dismissed by his descendants. Either way, however, the man knew how to prioritize, organize, and make the best use of his time without allowing hunger to stop him.

## TEA SANDWICHES

All of these sandwiches can be made at one time: Just have all the fixings ready and you'll be done in just a few minutes. English or hothouse cucumbers are crisper and sweeter than "regular," which need to be salted and drained of their bitter water. Seed and slice thin. If you're using a platter for the sandwiches, decorate it with a paper doily on the bottom and edible flowers all around. For a tiered tray, put one type of sandwich on each of the three tiers and garnish each plate with pieces of chives or edible flowers.

> 3 SLICES WHITE BREAD
> 3 SLICES WHOLE-WHEAT BREAD
> ¼ CUP (½ STICK) UNSALTED BUTTER, SOFTENED
> ¼ CUP MAYONNAISE
> 1 RIPE TOMATO, THINLY SLICED AND SEEDED
> 2 TABLESPOONS CHOPPED FRESH DILL
> 9–10 SLICES HOTHOUSE OR ENGLISH CUCUMBERS, SEEDED
> 1 CUP FRESH WATERCRESS
> ½ CUP CREAM CHEESE
> 4 WATER CRACKERS
> 2 SLICES SMOKED SALMON OR LOX
> 4 CHIVES, CUT INTO 1-INCH PIECES

1. Set out the slices of white bread in a row and lightly butter each slice. Set out the slices of wheat bread and lightly spread mayonnaise on them.
2. Place tomato slices on one slice of white bread. Cover with a second slice of white bread. Cut off the crusts. Cut the sandwich into quarters and dip the edges of the sandwiches in the chopped dill. Arrange on a plate.

3. Put the cucumbers on one slice of white bread and top with a slice of wheat bread. Trim the crust. Cut into two diagonal pieces and slice each of those in two so that you have four triangle-shaped sandwiches. Place them on the plate with the tomato sandwiches.

4. Blend the watercress with the cream cheese. Spread this mixture onto one slice of whole-wheat bread and top with another. Trim the crusts. Cut the bread into four equal rectangular slices. Place on the sandwich plate.

5. Lightly butter the crackers and put a piece of salmon on each, topped with a crisscross of chives.

6. If you do not serve immediately, cover the platter tightly with plastic wrap, and cover the wrap with a damp linen towel. Refrigerate until serving time.

*4 servings*

*Nothing is a better accompaniment to a sandwich than a cup of tea.*

## what goes with tea?

Teatime isn't necessarily sweet time. If you're feeling like a little snack but don't want "cakes and ices," consider dry-roasted nuts, plain crackers, and low-fat cheese, fresh fruit, or dried fruits (such as dates, raisins, or apricots.) Everything tastes better with a good cup of tea. Whether a solo tea or with guests, always serve snacks in pretty bowls; a careful presentation is part of the charm of teatime, and you should treat yourself as well as you treat your guests.

## EARL GREY TRUFFLES

A chocoholic's delight, these unusual truffles were developed by Chef Robert Wemischner of Los Angeles, a pioneer in the art of cooking with tea. The complexity of their flavor is based on a bergamot-scented Darjeeling tea infused by the cream, and the fruity flavor of the tea is further mellowed by the candied orange peel. For the most irresistible result, high-quality bittersweet chocolate works best (French Valrhona bittersweet is a good choice). A dusting of fine, pure dark bittersweet cocoa powder coats each square of creamy chocolate.

This is obviously more than enough for a foursome for tea, so wrap up extras in waxed paper and put them in little tins for your guests to take home; they'll be so grateful. *Note:* These may be made a day in advance and kept refrigerated until serving.

> STRIPS OF PEEL FROM 1 ORANGE
> 1 CUP WATER
> ½ CUP SUGAR
> 16 OUNCES HEAVY CREAM
> 2 TABLESPOONS EARL GREY IMPERIAL TEA LEAVES OR OTHER HIGH-GRADE EARL GREY
> 21 OUNCES BITTERSWEET CHOCOLATE, FINELY CHOPPED
> BITTERSWEET COCOA POWDER FOR DUSTING

1. Make candied orange peels by cutting strips from one brightly colored orange, making sure no white inner pith is used (the pith will make it bitter). Boil the peel in water for 5 minutes and drain. Boil again in fresh water and drain.
2. Make a simple syrup by boiling the water with the sugar until clear. Cook the peel for a third time in this simple syrup for about 5 minutes. Set aside.

3. In a heavy 2-quart saucepan, bring the cream and tea leaves to a boil. Remove from the heat and strain through a fine sieve into a bowl.

4. Add the chocolate and stir lightly with a wooden spoon until the chocolate is melted and the mixture is perfectly smooth. To retain its characteristic dense, fudgy texture, do not over-beat the chocolate mixture.

5. Puree the candied orange peel in a food processor along with approximately 1 cup of the chocolate mixture.

6. Line a pan measuring 8 inches by 10 inches by ¾ inches with baking parchment. Pour half of the remaining chocolate mixture into the pan. Pour all of the orange peel and chocolate mixture over the chocolate in the pan and spread evenly with a spatula. Pour the remaining chocolate mixture over this layer. Smooth the top with a spatula and cover tightly with baking parchment. Chill until firm, about 2 hours.

7. Remove from the refrigerator and prepare for serving by cutting the chilled chocolate with a heavy knife into 1-inch pieces. Place the pieces on a parchment-lined sheet pan and sift the cocoa powder over them, coating lightly and evenly. Place the truffles in small candy cups, if desired, and arrange them on a platter.

8. Refrigerate until 10 minutes before serving. These are best served cold, but not rock solid, because their flavor opens up after a few minutes at room temperature.

*about 72 bite-sized truffles*

(The crudités, dips, and tossed salad are American accents, to be sure, to round out the meal and make your mother happy that you're eating your vegetables. Recipes for those dishes are not included here.)

## MONDAY-NIGHT FOOTBALL HIGH TEA

It's the chill of winter, Monday-night football is the main entertainment, what's a person to do? Have tea, of course. High tea was and is a supper, one with leftover meats, Cornish pasties or shepherd's pie, and lots of hearty black tea. The word *high* may or may not have come from those high-backed chairs or Windsor chairs so many people owned. The other, more probable, source is the high table that a high tea is served at, rather than the low coffee or butler's table of an afternoon tea. In the north of England, even today, if you ask someone for tea you'll get a light meal at 6 P.M. that might consist of Cornish pasties, tea, and a dessert.

Football fans don't *have* to have potato chips, pizza, and beer. They can enjoy a satisfying meal, full of delicious, filling foods and the best darn tea they've ever had.

### Creating Ambience

Comfort is mandatory, so bring out plenty of pillows and some ottomans for relaxing the feet. If you can, two televisions would double the fun. Put one set in the buffet area and the other in the living room, so no one ever misses a touchdown, fumble, pass, or cheerleader.

### Setting the Table

A buffet is an absolute must; it will give your guests a chance to move around, and will make the event and the ensuing cleanup easy for you. Paper napkins and paper plates in your team's colors will also facilitate cleanup. Add a pennant or two in lieu of a vase of flowers, and a colorful paper tablecloth or cloth runners make a festive table.

Give each guest a mug with your favorite team's logo. It not only will help keep the tea hot, but also makes a thoughtful memento for guests to take home. Buy a few extra mugs and use them for silverware and napkin caddies.

# CORNISH PASTIES

READY-MADE PIECRUST DOUGH

1 POUND COOKED BEEF, DICED

1 CUP RAW POTATOES, DICED

1 CUP FINE-CHOPPED ONIONS

½ TEASPOON THYME

¼ TEASPOON FRESHLY GROUND BLACK PEPPER

1 TEASPOON SEA SALT OR KOSHER SALT

6 TABLESPOONS (¾ STICK) UNSALTED BUTTER

6 TABLESPOONS FRESH PARSLEY, CHOPPED

1 EGG YOLK, BEATEN

1 TABLESPOON WATER

1. Preheat the oven to 325°F.
2. Roll out the premade dough and cut into six 5-inch rounds.
3. Mix together the beef, potatoes, onions, thyme, pepper, and salt.
4. Spoon 3 tablespoons of the mixture on the south side of each circle; dot each with 1 tablespoon of butter and 1 tablespoon of parsley.
5. Moisten the edges of the pastry with water and fold over into the shape of a half circle or turnover, crimping the edges together with a fork.
6. Mix the egg yolk with the water and brush on each pasty.
7. Prick the top of each turnover with a fork.
8. Bake on a cookie sheet for 1 hour. Serve immediately.

*6 servings*

## the tea

To stand up to the hearty entrées in this high tea, consider the brisk, biting taste of a Kenyan tea. This black tea is very forgiving, can be brewed for up to 5 minutes, and tastes just as vigorous on the second steeping. Other choices are an Indian Assam, a Chinese Yunnan, or a blend such as Irish Breakfast.

# SHEPHERD'S PIE

This is a simple dish to use up leftover Sunday "joint" or roast beef dinner in the north of England, and something typically eaten on a Monday. That's why it's a great match for your Monday-Night Football High Tea.

2 CUPS MINCED ROAST BEEF
1 CUP COOKED CARROTS
1 CUP GREEN PEAS
½ CUP COOKED ONIONS
2 CUPS COOKED MASHED POTATOES
1 CUP CHEDDAR CHEESE, GRATED

1. Preheat the broiler.
2. Combine the roast beef, carrots, peas, and onions.
3. Spread the beef mixture over the bottom of a 9-inch by 12-inch glass or ceramic dish. Then spread a thick layer of the mashed potatoes on top and, with a fork, draw lines down the pan.
4. Sprinkle the cheese on the top and broil for about 10 minutes or until the mashed potatoes are browned. Serve immediately.

*6 servings*

*Fresh vegetables make for a delicious Shepherd's Pie.*

## SHORTBREAD

1 CUP (2 STICKS) UNSALTED BUTTER, SOFTENED
¾ CUP ALL-PURPOSE WHITE FLOUR
¾ CUP RICE FLOUR
½ CUP SUGAR

1. Preheat the oven to 325˚F.
2. Cream the butter with a hand mixer.
3. In a second bowl, sift together the two flours with the sugar, then blend in the butter until you have a buttery yellow, light batter. Pour into a shallow 8-inch square pan and score with a knife into eight even squares.
4. Bake for 20 minutes or until golden brown. You may cut the shortbread while hot, but allow the pieces to cool completely before removing from the pan.

*9 servings*

## loose leaf or bags?

You'll get more flavor, more cups per teaspoon, and more value for your money with loose-leaf tea. You don't really need a lot of gadgets and gewgaws; good tea naturally sinks to the bottom of the pot, but any inexpensive bamboo or wire-mesh strainer will catch the errant leaf. If convenience is your goal, then certainly consider all the high-quality tea bag brands on your grocer's shelf. Experiment with different types and flavors of tea. Tea is an adventure to be explored.

## PROTOCOL TEA FOR LEARNING MANNERS

Children as young as three can begin to learn the simple gestures of good manners, such as saying please and thank-you. As they begin to build their vocabularies and learn how to communicate in complete sentences, they can learn other forms of manners — for example, how to play nicely with other children on the playground, and how to greet adults and children they visit.

Each step toward civility is a building block you provide your children that will bring enormous benefits of increased confidence, assurance, and the ability to be amid any group at any time and feel in command of themselves. Basic good manners need not evolve into the complexity of diplomatic protocol, but every possible experience we can provide our children will make them more congenial, accomplished adults.

One of the most amazing elements of a traditional tea party for children is that they instinctively turn on their best behavior. Ask anyone who hosts children's tea parties; they'll tell you that breakage, misbehavior, and rudeness are almost unheard of. When presented to children as a form of playing grown-up, learning good manners is enormous fun. Just don't tell them it's good for them.

*A miniature tea set is the delight of many a young tea-party hostess.*

### Creating Ambience

The ambience of the room and the dress for the children should be "Sunday best." Before the party, instruct your children on how to greet and welcome their guests; open the door and welcome each person; thank them for coming; take their coats and hang them up; and escort their guests to the tea party area and introduce them to other guests.

This party is geared for children age 7 through 10, so sitting at an adult-sized table is entirely appropriate, and will be another signal to them that they are now "grown up enough" to do what the adults do when having tea.

*Note:* If the guests have never been to a tea party before, or are new to formal dining, the parent of the hosts or another adult should offer gentle advice and instruction. These instructions can include:

- Greetings for hosts and guests
- How to start a conversation and what subjects to talk about (such as vacations, games they like, or books and videos they enjoy)
- How to use the utensils
- How to pour tea and serve platters
- How to eat the foods and drink from cups
- How to say thank-yous and good-byes

## Setting the Table

Use china dinnerware and regular silverware, porcelain teacups and saucers, and linen napkins. Beside each child's plate should be a place card made by your children, plus a favor that can be geared to their ages or interests. Some ideas for favors are tussy mussies or other flowers for the girls and handmade tea bags with the guests' names on them. Any little toy or game suited to the age group, from marbles to puzzles, will also be appreciated.

The supervising adults can pour the first cups of tea and bring the meal to the table; then the child hosts can pour second cups and pass around plates for second helpings, following the waiter style of serving to the right and taking from the left. Rehearse how to pour and serve several times prior to the tea to give them experience and confidence with these new skills.

Other gestures of protocol you might include are teaching boys to pull out chairs for the girls, opening and closing doors for entering and exiting guests, shaking hands when saying hello and goodbye, and bowing and curtseying. The last suggestion may sound very formal, but children love to do it

So, now for a feast,
Bread and jam at the least,
And there's cake on a dish
For those who may wish;
Milk and water and sugar
and very weak tea.

— ELIZA KEARY,
"At Home Again" (1883)

# CHOCOLATE-COVERED STRAWBERRIES

For this recipe, make sure strawberries are both thoroughly cleaned and thoroughly dried. If there is too much moisture on them, the chocolate will not adhere properly to them. You know what to do with the leftover chocolate . . .

16 OUNCES MILK CHOCOLATE

36 LARGE STRAWBERRIES, PICKED CLEAN OF DEBRIS, LIGHTLY RINSED, AND DRIED THOROUGHLY

1. Melt the chocolate in the top of a double boiler, stirring constantly. When the chocolate has melted completely, remove from the heat and place on the counter.

2. Taking each strawberry by its green stem, dip it completely in the chocolate, then lay it on its side on waxed paper. Repeat until all the strawberries have been completely covered in chocolate.

3. Allow the strawberries to cool, then carefully place them on a decorative platter, cover with waxed paper or foil, and refrigerate until ready to serve. Let them sit for about 10 minutes at room temperature before eating. Place with a bowl to catch the stems.

*18 two-strawberry servings*

*Fresh strawberries are a delicious
and nutritious treat for children.*

## LEMON COOKIES

This is a refreshing cookie from an original recipe created by my *TEA TALK* food columnist, Gary Stotsky.

1 CUP (2 STICKS) UNSALTED BUTTER

1 CUP SUGAR

2 LARGE EGGS

1 TEASPOON BAKING SODA

3 CUPS FLOUR

6 OUNCES UNDILUTED, THAWED LEMONADE, FROM FROZEN CONCENTRATE

1. Preheat the oven to 400°F.
2. Cream together the butter and the sugar until they're a soft yellow color.
3. Add the eggs one at a time, beating after each addition.
4. In a separate bowl, sift together the baking soda and flour. Sift the dry ingredients a second time directly into the egg mixture along with 2 ounces of the lemonade. Stir thoroughly.
5. Drop the batter onto an ungreased cookie sheet with a teaspoon, leaving about 2 inches between each cookie.
6. Bake on the top rack of the oven until the edges are lightly browned, about 8 minutes.
7. Remove from the oven and, while still warm, brush the cookies lightly with the remaining lemonade.

*about 24 cookies*

**the tea**

To make a tasty yet not too strong tea for children, combine equal parts English Breakfast tea and milk.

# Peanut Butter Muffins

4 CUPS UNBLEACHED WHITE FLOUR

2 TEASPOONS BAKING SODA

2 TEASPOONS BAKING POWDER

½ CUP SMOOTH PEANUT BUTTER

4 LARGE EGGS

1 BANANA

⅔ CUP CANOLA OR GRAPESEED OIL

2 CUPS MILK

1 CUP CHOPPED PEANUTS

1 CUP SEMISWEET CHOCOLATE CHIPS OR MORSELS

1. Preheat the oven to 350°F. Grease and flour enough muffin tins to make 24 regular-sized muffins or 48 mini muffins.
2. In a bowl, sift together the flour, baking soda, and baking powder.
3. In a second bowl, beat together the peanut butter with the eggs and banana, until creamy. Add the oil and milk and beat for at least another minute.
4. Slowly add the dry ingredients to the wet, mixing well. Gently fold in the peanuts and chocolate chips.
5. Fill each muffin cup about three-quarters full.
6. Bake for about 15 minutes or until lightly brown.

*24 regular-sized or 48 mini muffins*

looking into
the future
with tea

*Matrons, who toss the cup, and see*
*The grounds of fate in grounds of tea . . .*
— ALEXANDER POPE (1688–1744)

reading tea leaves, like reading coffee grounds, is an ancient art practiced by thousands for centuries. While it is easy to learn the general rules of tasseography, it may take a lifetime to understand the effects of interpreting the leaves for your audience. Reading tea leaves takes sympathy, empathy, consideration, and sincerity, and should not be entered into lightly; it carries a good deal of responsibility.

## FORTUNE TEA

Tea leaves hold many truths for those ready to learn. Invite likeminded friends to a Fortune Tea and share the signs of health, wealth, and love that point the way to their tomorrows.

### Creating Ambience

To begin, both the tea leaf reader, or tasseographer, and the client must be comfortable. Padded seats with supportive backs and a cloth-covered table in a quiet, intimately sized area are essential. Your Victorian Folding Screen (see page 18) would make a discreet enclosure. Tea leaf reading is a private, personal relationship, and boundaries must be respected.

If this is an evening experience, place some lighted candles on the table to illuminate the leaves and give a softer, lovelier feeling than an ordinary electric lamp can.

During the daytime, the garden is a good setting for a tea leaf reading, especially when you're surrounded by flowers, comfortable chairs, and a nicely set table. Allow a good ten to fifteen minutes for each reading. The leaves have *much* to tell!

## READING THE LEAVES
## THE EUROPEAN WAY

After finishing a cup of tea, the fate seeker turns the teacup upside down on the saucer, and turns the cup around three times in a counterclockwise direction with his left hand. He will end with the handle of the teacup facing the tea leaf reader.

Holding the saucer with her left hand and the bottom of the cup in her right hand, the tea leaf reader turns the cup over, taking care not to move the configurations of the tea leaves. Now that the cup is again on its saucer, the tea leaf reader can study the shapes of the leaves that have remained, identify the symbols they have formed, and give an interpretation.

### Interpreting the Symbols

Where the leaves cling in the cup is a critical part of determining their meaning. For example, if the leaves are close to the handle, that indicates something about home and family. However, if the leaves land opposite the handle, the reading is about something away from home, or strangers in the fate seeker's life.

Leaves on the right side of the handle signal events and people coming into life; leaves on the left side signal the departure of people and end of events. If the tea leaves are near the brim, the events are to happen in the near future, but if the leaves are located on the bottom, events will occur farther into the future, perhaps as much as a year or more.

When interpreting the images, let your intuition give you clues to definitions. The variation of the shapes are nearly limitless. Here are interpretations of some of the most common symbols.

*Tea-leaf formations inside a cup can take many shapes.*

*bell*

*dagger*

*fish*

*mushroom*

*spider*

# A Guide to Common Tasseography Symbols

| IMAGE | MEANING |
|---|---|
| acorn | at the top of the cup, success and gain; at the bottom of the cup, good health |
| angels | good news, always |
| aircraft | journey; if broken, danger of accident; can also indicate a rise in position |
| anchor | at the top of the cup, stability; at the bottom of the cup, restlessness |
| bell | good news, especially if it's near the top of the cup |
| birds | messengers of good news |
| boat | visit from a friend; protection |
| book | if open, good news; if closed, search your heart for feelings |
| circle | a sign of the continuum, marital rings, happiness, or the successful completion of something |
| clouds | something exciting is coming to stir things up; sometimes happy surprises, sometimes sad ones; the darker the formation, the more serious it is |
| cup | reward |
| dagger | danger from self or others; beware |
| dish | trouble at home |
| dog | good friend; if at the bottom of the cup, the friend needs help |
| door | odd event |
| egg | new beginning; possibly impending birth of a baby or an idea |
| elephant | strength and wisdom |
| fence | temporary limitations or minor setbacks |
| fish | good fortune to come (not necessarily money) |
| flowers | signs of happiness |
| grapes (bunch) | much happiness from many sources |
| gun | a caution; not necessarily danger, but anger |

| | |
|---|---|
| hammer | a tool you need to do the hard work ahead |
| hand | if closed like a fist, conflict; if open, the pleasure of friendship |
| heart | love and pleasure you can trust and enjoy for many years to come |
| hourglass | time to make that decision; no more putting it off |
| house | shelter; security is coming your way |
| kite | your deepest wishes will come true |
| ladder | another level in your life; another promotion at work; another triumph |
| leaf | a new life; if many are shown, abundance and intensity in both family and work life; one leaf near the rim, money is coming |
| lines | straight and even, progress; zigzag, ups and downs and uncertainty ahead |
| mountain | prepare to climb; your goals are in sight but obstacles are, too |
| mushroom | at the bottom of the cup, rapid growth; at the top of the cup, movement (such as a journey or a move); if it is upside down, however, frustration and disruption |
| question mark | the worry sign; take caution |
| ring | marriage or strong relationship; breaks mean only for a short while |
| scissors | possible separation; the farther apart the blades, the longer the separation |
| ship | travel is on the horizon |
| snake | wisdom; or a potential enemy |
| spider | with a web close to it, substantial reward for hard work; no web, keep on working and the goal will be forthcoming |
| spoon | you'll soon be served great generosity |
| star | health and happiness |
| sun | the light of happiness will soon be yours |
| tree | depending on the fullness of the shape, improvements; sturdy or weak characteristics are to be noted |
| triangle | something unexpected, usually with three parts |
| wheel | completely formed, good fortune ahead; broken, temporary breaks |
| wings | a messenger is coming with something you need to hear; listen! |

## the tea

Any tea can be read in the cup, but loose Indian teas such as Assam are preferable, because the leaves are larger. If you only have ground tea leaves, do not despair, for that can give you vivid images of a different sort.

## READING THE LEAVES THE PAN-ASIAN WAY

This is a rarely used format, but one I have adapted to great success. It requires a Chinese *guywan,* or covered cup with saucer. The saucer is used to steady the cup, the cup holds the future, and the lid or cover is used for viewing the past. Any type of tea can be used, but a ground black tea is preferred, such as that from tea bags or hearty rough broken leaves.

The tasseographer (tea leaf reader) pours about 2 tablespoons of tea from a teapot into the *guywan* and asks the client to turn the entire cup around three times to the left and three times to the right. Placing the entire *guywan* in the left hand (which links to the heart) and covering the top of it with the right hand (which links to the soul), the client turns the *guywan* upside down three times over a tea drainer, then sets the *guywan* down between himself and the

*The client turns the guywan upside down three times before the leaves are read.*

reader. With her right hand, the reader lifts off the lid and sets it upside down to the right of the cup. The inside of the lid will never look the same as it did before; still, it tells much about the past: sorrows, joys, a clean slate, or confusion.

### Interpreting the Symbols

The cup itself holds three stories: the immediate present, indicated by shapes and forms near the edge of the rim of the cup; what is in the immediate future for money, love, health, and interests on the sides of the cup; and, finally, the general future, located at the absolute bottom of the cup. The saucer is used to keep the cup steady; it allows the reader to turn the cup without touching it and interfering with the aura infused by the client.

Much of what the reader looks for is degrees of intensity, amounts, direction, and strengths and weaknesses. Here are just a few examples of the various symbols, shapes, and intuitive glimpses into the tea leaf reader's cup.

Mounds of tea, especially those piled up, indicate unresolved questions that may be personal, professional, or intellectual. It is not uncommon to see many mounds in the cups of philosophers, scientists, mathematicians, or other problem solvers. For many other people this could indicate lingering feelings about moves, separations, losses, and other natural changes that occur in all our lives.

If there are a number of mounds on the lid, it can very well impact the future. The ideal image is mounds on the sides with a clear opening between them. This formation indicates that the client is ready to enter the future with enthusiasm and energy. A clear lid means a clear past.

In the cup, mounds of tea indicate passion and intensity. This could be an abundance of love, work, and friendship. When related to money, the mounds mean huge power and wealth. However, in the area of health (on the right side of the cup) mounds indicate serious illness and must be addressed immediately.

It is not unusual to have no tea in one or several areas. That simply means a state of limbo, a quiet time, a peace for the moment. When the teas are primarily along the rim of the cup, results will be forthcoming most likely in weeks or months. Teas clinging to the sides of the cup and headed toward the bottom indicate that the results are definitely in the future.

*The future can be read through the location and shape of the leaves in the cup.*

The very bottom of the cup and the lid may or may not have tea liquor in it. When there is an abundance of tea liquid it means joy and happiness, lightness, warmth. The absence does not mean the absence of joy; it just means that joy will not be the overriding element of the near future.

Tea leaves on the bottom of the cup naturally fall into a circle. How that circle appears can be interpreted this way: A full covered circle means an intense, busy, excited life with a strong integration of personal and professional roles; a sharp division between two areas in the circle means a river of joy divides your outside interests and your home life; scattered, broken areas with lots of liquor or space between mean a future with many, many involvements, all of which may be separate from one another. This can be very lively or distracting, depending upon the person.

# part three
## TEA IN THE GARDEN

*Come, prithee make it up, Miss, and be as lovers be,*
*We'll go to Bagnigge Wells, Miss, and there we'll have some tea;*
*It's there you'll see the lady-birds perched on the stinging nettles,*
*And Chrystal water fountains, and shining copper kettles;*
*It's there you'll see the fishes, more curious they than whales,*
*They're made of gold and silver, Miss, and wags their little tails.*
— MR. CHURCHILL, IN *AMUSEMENT OF OLD LONDON* (1779)

One of the most amazing facts about living on a floating home is how important gardening has become to me and all my neighbors. Here we are with no lawns to mow, no weeds to dig up, no snails, bugs, deer, or wayward pets to demolish the grass, yet the need to touch earth is still with us. We sway with the winds like babes in a cradle most days, have views of white-tipped sailboats and brilliant-colored kayaks gliding over the bay like skaters on ice. Sometimes we set sail ourselves, but it's not necessary to be farther out to sea when you're already floating right on top of it.

So why this craving for plants? From the beginning to the end of the long winding dock that serves as a walkway between two rows of houseboats are trees, bushes, plants, flowers, herbs, and fruit trees. One neighbor is a particularly gifted gardener, and her cymbidiums are legend: silky, long lasting, glorious. I pluck one (with her permission, of course) and keep it in a huge brandy glass of water, where it floats serenely in the middle of my tea table. I can either look out at ducks on the bay or gaze down at this exquisite, exotic bloom while sipping an afternoon cup of tea.

The wild pepper scent of nasturtiums begs to be added to the dinner salad. What fun it would be to throw a petal or two into my next cup of chai instead of the traditional ground black pepper. Continuing my walk along the dock, I smell fragrant thyme, which adds such a twist to iced tea, and pungent rosemary, perfect with a roasted chicken. Long stalks of lavender with their fuzzy-soft ends have countless uses: Strew a few petals instead of bergamot in a cup of Earl Grey tea, or use them as a natural addition to dream pillows — so relaxing a scent placed by my bed pillow, or lovely on the nightstand.

Old English roses with that nearly indefinable scent stand magnificently in their blushing pinks and soft yellows among young upstarts of silver and multihues bred for drama. Tinier roses, actually called tea roses, can be placed in my cup of Keemun or Assam black for just a hint of fragrance and that sweet, silky taste roses bring to water.

The oranges on our tiny tree are quite small and delicately sweet; a few scrapes of the zest and any black tea, hot or iced, tastes extra special. The tomatoes, also small, are each perfect, with much less trace of acid than their on-land counterparts. Cacti and succulents (California really is a desert, honest!), lilies and geraniums and pansies, all stick up their colorful heads to say hello and vie for the attention of residents and guests.

Plants here thrive indoors as well. The gigantic fern has died several times from being set too close to the overenthusiastic heating fan, yet its magnificent gossamer leaves are resurrected by noontime the next day with a cooling respite on the back deck and an extra dose of leftover tea and spent tea leaves laid on the dirt. The other green plants lap up the sun from never-covered windows and seem to not need the typical heliotropic turn, because there is sunlight everywhere.

Upstairs, downstairs, front deck, top deck, outside dock, plants are everywhere. They thrive because it is natural for humans to touch plants and earth, absorbing the lovely fragrances of flowers, the sweetness of fresh fruits, and the pungency of fresh-cut herbs. And yes, they are all fed leftover tea liquor and the infused leaves, and yes, it really, *really* does help.

In the dining room/tearoom is a meditation corner where a bamboo screen and tall plants offer shade, a man-made rock fountain tinkles gently, and several pillows and a well-worn kilim rug offer comfort atop the polished hardwood floors. Here I sit each morning with my Darjeeling, inhaling its bouquet, thinking or not thinking about the day ahead. In the evening, I sit in the darkened room with just one candle burning to accompany my tea making. This time, I pour a delicate white or green into a tiny Chinese cup, savoring each sip as if it were my first. Sometimes the peace and tranquillity is so like a warm blanket around me I feel a loss that the candle must be extinguished, the cup put away, so that I can go to my bed. Still, I do believe this tradition of respite in my indoor "tea garden" is one of the most treasured gifts I have received from this most remarkable beverage called tea.

So here I am, living on water and yet gardening as if I am on land. Why this need for a garden? Perhaps gardens are a symbol of completeness, from dust to dust; or perhaps it's the theory that we get necessary minerals by osmosis when we garden in rich earth. Maybe this desire lingers just because it's so pretty to see a flower, so lovely to taste fruit grown from seed or herbs cut fresh whenever you need them. Maybe it's so essential that there really is no reason to ask why.

I do so hope you have a spot for a garden. Even if you have room only for a window box of flowers, a trailing sweet potato plant or tin of herbs in the kitchen, or a square-foot lot in the backyard for vegetables, you'll discover that happiness grows more abundantly when you grow a garden. Like all beautiful things, plants and flowers offer you something pretty to see, to help you daydream while sipping a cup of warm, nourishing tea. What a wonderful combination of two worlds: tea and the garden.

# creating a tea garden

Savoring the brief periods of lovely summertime weather amid the beauty of flowers and plants was the beginning of entertaining with tea in London gardens. This tradition reached its height in the 17th and 18th centuries in a style that seems both quaint and timeless. We are just as likely today to celebrate with music, fireworks, and entertainment as the Londoners did centuries ago in these sylvan amusement parks. "Breakfasting as well as the evening entertainment of ladies and gentlemen" were part of the day's events, along with simple foods like bread and butter, some cakes and sweets, ale, coffee, chocolate, and the still fairly new beverage, tea.

## TEA GARDENS IN ENGLAND

The enthusiasm for the pleasure garden grew in large part because they were festive, and welcomed women and families and lovers. You could stroll down fragrant floral walkways, sip tea (or steal a kiss) under shaded arbors, play on the bowling greens or skittle grounds, dance to music in the great rooms, or exercise the panic of the heart with gambling at the tables or racetracks.

### Vauxhall Gardens

Perhaps the most famous of the 17th- and 18th-century pleasure gardens was Vauxhall Gardens, to which you could ride in a small boat down to the south bank of the Thames, disembarking to walk the short distance east of Vauxhall Bridge. No less a personage than Frederic, Prince of Wales, attended the opening fete and set the tone for what would become a very popular and sophisticated garden. Created by Johnathan Typers in 1732, Vauxhall was sparkle and glamour amid lantern-lit walks, dramatic fireworks, and an elaborate bandstand designed in the Gothic style — a dramatic backdrop for the most popular bands and singers of the day.

For a shilling, you could stay for hours and enjoy a celebratory atmosphere from breakfast tea to nighttime concerts. From 1750 to 1790, Vauxhall welcomed royalty, aristocrats, and the stars of the literary set, including Horace Walpole, that "hardened and shameless tea-drinker" Dr. Samuel Johnson, and Henry Fielding, who wrote that "love and scandal are the best sweeteners for tea" in his charming tale *Love in Several Masques* (1743).

## Ranelagh Gardens

Essayist Horace Walpole wrote much about this era; about Ranelagh he wrote, "There is a vast amphitheater, finely gilt, painted and illuminated, into which everybody that loves eating, drinking, staring or crowding, is admitted for twelvepence." Billed as a place of public entertainment, Ranelagh opened in 1742 in Chelsea on the former home and grounds of the late earl of Ranelagh. Its famous Rotunda was the setting for the looking and "staring" that Walpole referred to in perhaps the first recorded remark on how some people love to see and be seen. The guests, literally, walked around and around the magnificent ornate colonnade in the center of this mammoth round room.

This "going 'round in circles" was the source of many satirical remarks, although poet Samuel Roers took the kinder view that Ranelagh was so still that "you could hear the whishing sound of ladies' trains as the immense assembly walked round and round the room."

*Traditional English tea gardens feature lush plantings and ornate furniture.*

## the legend of Emma Hart

Sometimes patrons got much more value for their small fee. No drama was more talked about nor the base of more legends than the story of the mistress of the Honorable Charles Greville.

After taking his leave of this young lady to visit some of his society friends, the gentleman was aghast to discover upon his return to their boxed seat that the young woman had a mind of her own. With unbridled bravado, and perhaps a little ale, she leaned out from the box in full view of the audience and burst into glorious song. The other attendees were thrilled with her performance and with the decidedly embarrassed countenance of Greville.

The young mistress was shortly thereafter abandoned by her "noble" lover, but not for long. She soon received a promotion of sorts, to Lady Hamilton, and became a strong presence in the very same society she had entertained as young Emma Hart, "the tea maker of Edgware Road."

Although a decided competitor of Vauxhall, Ranelagh had a less idyllic look with more activity areas and theatricality, a direct result of its theater-manager-turned-garden-director, Sir Thomas Robinson. Ranelagh's Rotunda housed an enormous fireplace to keep patrons warm on inclement evenings, and boxed seats for its more important, and wealthier, guests. The orchestra stand had a huge pipe organ, and an immense stage offered both performers and audience a magnificent arena for musical and dramatic entertainments.

Like Vauxhall, Ranelagh had a location near water, this time a small canal between tree-lined walks rather than the miles-long Thames. The smaller waterway did not stop the entrepreneurs, or the architects of the day, from building replicas of a Venetian temple and a Chinese house to give the park further drama.

Lovely gardens, fine tea and biscuits, and a dash of show biz were always available at Ranelagh, and all for only 2 shilling tuppence.

### Marylebone Gardens

London was not the only place where the English could enjoy the pleasure garden. The capital city's suburbs soon welcomed their own versions, particularly Marylebone, built by one Daniel Gough atop a former tavern and bowling alley on High Street in the early 1750s. It had the de rigueur great room for dances, supper parties, and theatrical performances, plus masked carnivals (ridottos) highlighted by the increasingly popular display of fireworks.

The garden's second owner, John Trusler, had a clever daughter who, instead of plain bread and butter, baked rich seed and plum cakes to serve with copious pots of tea. This change in the menu not only brought great pleasure to the guests, it also brought many shillings to the Truslers. The garden went through several other owners, yet people continued to come for the entertainment, occasional sword fight, and food until 1776, when it closed.

# TEA GARDENS IN AMERICA

Pleasure gardens were not limited to London and its suburbs; their tradition gained a gentle foothold in the New World. The most celebrated gardens were located in the New York and Boston areas.

## Tea Water Pump Garden

In New York, tea gardens commonly opened near springs, like Knapp's at 10th Avenue and 14th Street and also at Christopher Street and Sixth Avenue. Perhaps the most famous of them all was the Tea Water Pump Garden, located at a freshwater spring near Chatham (Park Row) and Roosevelt Streets.

The reason for the proximity to springs was that even in the 18th century, spring water was preferred over municipal water, so much so that the Corporation of New York installed a tea water pump where the Tea Water Pump Garden was built. "Carters" were hired to peddle the fresh spring water with noisy and exuberant cries of "Tea water! Tea water!" as up and down the streets they walked. Their tireless enthusiasm began to grate so much on the ears, and nerves, of nearby residents and businesses that the Common Council was forced to enact a regulation in 1757 restricting the presence, hours, and numbers of these tea men.

## Other New York Gardens

With the Revolutionary War tea drinking came to a decided halt for quite a while. In fact, it was not until 1828, with the opening of Sans Souci, that tea arrived in New York eating establishments once again. William Niblo's Sans Souci was quickly followed by Contoit's, the New York Garden, and Cherry Gardens. Then trends changed still again and tea gardens unfortunately fell into disuse for about 40 years, until with the 1920s and 1930s came the development of the tearoom as we know it today.

## other popular gardens

Many other gardens opened in England this era, some dignified, others boisterous. The music of Handel and Corelli often debuted at Cuper's Gardens (1691–1759), whose al fresco teas were supervised by Mrs. Ephriam Evans, a widow of one of the original owners and a clever businesswoman. She kept Cuper's open longer than any other owner had.

Artist Thomas Keyse added a health-giving spa to his garden, Bermondsey Spa Gardens, and used it extensively to display many of his canvases for patrons to admire and buy. Balloon rides were an occasional sight at White Conduit House, and Nell Gwynne and her many royal lovers were frequently seen at Bagnigge Wells.

These were but a few of the hundreds of small and medium-sized gardens that welcomed belles and their beaux and where, weather permitting, they could discreetly sip tea in a special spot on open lawns or under beautifully wrought pavilions. None remains.

## TEA IN THE MODERN GARDEN

In the summer of my 15th year, I discovered the intimacy of gardening. My family and I had moved to our own home, and in the backyard, practically hidden in the corner of the property among pine trees, was a very small Japanese tea garden, complete with a tiny koi pond, about 2 feet in diameter, regulation fire-engine red mini bridge, and faux teahouse— which, in the Pennsylvania of the late 1950s, was very, very exotic.

Now, whenever I think of tea and gardening, I recall the serenity and peace that have embraced me not only in the tiny Japanese tea garden of my childhood home, but in the many authentic Japanese tea gardens I have visited in person, and over and over again in books with dramatic photographs of lush green, serene gardens.

### Classic Japanese Tea Garden (Roji)

A tea garden is a walk through time and space, designed to prepare you to receive a bowl of tea in peace and serenity. To someone new to the Japanese tea garden, it can appear empty and still, its design one of controlled manipulation, void of the free range of nature left unchained. That feeling is fully intended, for it is the visitors who bring life to the Japanese tea garden, even as they sit quietly on simple benches set between moss and stone. Preston L. Houser writes that the Japanese tea garden is a metaphor for spiritual awakening: By the time you arrive at the teahouse you are already on the "other shore."

In the tradition of Buddhism, the garden around a tearoom is *arawa,* "disclosure," as in disclosing the body and soul to purify yourself before entering the tearoom. Above all, a Japanese tea garden is sensual, exquisitely scenic, restful, and nourishing to the spirit. To foster this journey from the outside world to the inner world of tea, the garden should include a bench for resting, a stone-studded path, and plants and trees that encourage meditation.

All are deliberately placed; the elements of chance or serendipity have no place here. The design of stone-studded paths is particularly interesting. They are rarely straight, and great care is taken when determining the height and distance of one stone from another. They must be set close enough to offer a pleasant visual pattern, yet far enough apart to slow down the visitor's pace en route to the teahouse.

Carrying a wooden bucket of spring water, the host freshens plants and trees, cleans the stepping-stones his guests will follow to his tea gathering, and sprinkles water around the garden as a purifying gesture. He also cleans his hands and mouth, as do the guests, prior to entering the teahouse. This implies wiping the mind clean of illusion, discarding prejudices, so that all can enter the tearoom free of what the Buddhists deem the three realms of existence: the past, the present, and the future. It is a profound gesture of making the body and soul pure to accept a bowl of tea.

*A teahouse is set on the edge of a pond in this splendid Japanese garden.*

**LEVEL OF EXPERTISE:**
easy

**TOOLS AND MATERIALS:**
small wooden rake

½–1 inch deep picture frame

sand or gravel

a few seashells or rocks from
   your favorite walks

a very small bonsai plant in
   its own container
   (optional)

# PORTABLE ZEN GARDEN

No space is too small for a spiritual entryway. If you have no backyard or garden space, bring the peaceful tea garden inside your home. Create a mini rock garden to place on a table, outside on a small patio, or even in a flower box in lieu of flowers.

You can make or buy a Zen garden, one that duplicates the traditional full-sized exterior garden of sand, gravel, and carefully placed rocks and trees. All you need to display it is about a 12-inch square space, such as you would find on the edge of a hearth or coffee table.

Put the Zen garden at one end and your tea accoutrements at the other. Now, next time you take your tea, you can sit and relax, sip a delicate green sencha or gyokuro tea, and "tend" your garden. Rake the sand into shapes and mounds to suit your mood. Discover how serene a place you have created for yourself with a personal Zen garden.

1. On a table or counter, lay the picture frame face up. Carefully pour in a 1-inch or deeper layer of sand or gravel.

2. Use the rake to create lines or curves in the sand or gravel.

3. Place the rocks or seashells in a pleasing pattern. Add the bonsai plant, if desired.

*Step 3: After raking lines into the sand, place your rocks in a visually pleasing design.*

## SERENITY TERRARIUM

If potted plants and greenery are more your style than the simplicity of rocks and gravel, make a Serenity Terrarium — a garden in a fishbowl.

Position your Serenity Terrarium in such a way that, while sipping tea, you can see its infinitely rewarding and satisfying view, and you'll experience a lovely sense of calm.

1. Place your gravel and charcoal mixture in the bottom of the container. Lay the netting or sheet moss on top of that.

2. Top with soil mixture, then the ground cover (if using one).

3. Make small depressions in the soil. Place the plants in the depressions, and firmly mound up the roots with soil. Cover area around the plants with spent tea leaves for additional fertilizing.

4. Decorate with rocks, pebbles, shells, or miniature tea accessories.

5. Water the entire terrarium very evenly and slowly, allowing the water to steep in completely. If the bowl is kept at a room temperature of 65 to 80 °F, there should be enough humidity for the plants to need only rare watering.

**Step 4:** *Add your decorations to the planted terrarium.*

LEVEL OF EXPERTISE:
easy

TOOLS AND MATERIALS:
glass container such as a fishbowl, large brandy snifter, small aquarium tank, or even a Waterford bowl

3 parts gravel to one part charcoal

soil separator of nylon netting, nylon stockings, or sheet moss

soil mixture of 1 part *each* sand and Black Magic Planter mix with 2 parts potting soil or garden soil

plants: philodendron, nasturtium, mimosa, osmanthus, African violet, small ferns, or miniature begonia, and ground cover such as coral bead plant (*Nertera depressa*) or string of hearts (*Ceropegia woddii*)

spent tea leaves

decorative touches such as pebbles, shells, miniature teacups and teapots

# MEDITATION IN THE GARDEN

The garden holds magic for many of us: the beauty of all the growing plants, the flutter of a summer butterfly, the nesting of a family of birds, the warmth of the sun during the day, and the glow of stars at night.

We meditate in a garden each in our own way whenever we inhale the life-giving oxygen plants give off. No matter what size your garden is, every visit can be an enhancing, meditative experience. Sit in a comfortable chair, lie on the grass or on a chaise lounge, and savor this time alone with the simple gifts of nature.

## Exercises

To ease you from the cares of the day into your garden temple, take a cup of tea with you. Sip slowly, taste the tea anew, enjoy everything about tea that you love.

As you view the garden, empty your mind of the everyday demands and ease into a meditative state. Try this simple yoga exercise:

1. With your eyes closed, breathe in as deeply as you can, counting slowly to four

2. Hold your breath for the count of seven

3. Slowly, slowly exhale your breath for the count of eight

4. Repeat these steps three more times

5. Now, open your eyes.

Everything should look more vivid, more vital. Your body will feel genuinely relaxed and able to take in more of the loveliness around you. Visit your garden as often as you can.

# tips for using tea around the garden

WILDFLO
Perennial Mi
Mixed Colors and Kin

WILDFLO
Perennial Mi

*The true gardener . . . brushes over the ground with
slow and gentle hands, to liberate a space
for breath round some favourite.*
— FREYDA STARK, FROM *PERSEUS IN THE WIND* (1948)

t hroughout this book I have given occasional hints for using tea leaves and tea liquor. Now I want to end the book as tea ends, by going back to the earth, to replenish, nourish, recycle in every good sense of the word.

Tea is the most remarkably biodegradable plant in the world. It quenches our thirst, adds sparkle to our food, inspires art, literature, and music, helps us heal and nourish our bodies as it comforts our souls. Spent tea leaves or leftover tea are excellent sources of nutrients when fed to your houseplants; in fact, tea is a "quality food" for any plant, flower, tree, or herb in your backyard.

Just as you had fun with projects inside, you can have a ball decorating outside with tea. Here are a few of my favorite projects.

## Barbecue with Tea

Smoking adds a distinctive aroma to tea, and a smoky-tasting tea like Lapsang Souchong or Russian Caravan adds a hearty aroma to food. You can use the tea directly in food or add it to the wood or charcoal fuel in your barbecue grill. Sprinkle about 1 cup of fresh unsteeped tea leaves on the fuel. The aroma of the tea will steep into the grilled meats, poultry, and vegetables for an extra punch. Fruit-flavored black teas, such as peach, passion fruit, or apple-cinnamon, add a touch of spice to poultry, if the smoky taste is not for you.

## Easy Mosquito Repellent

Allow your spent tea leaves to dry overnight. When thoroughly dry, put them into metal trays or ashtrays and light a match to them. If needed, add a small piece of burning charcoal briquette to the leaves. This "tea incense" generates enough tea aroma to drive mosquitoes away. Any unscented, unflavored tea will do.

## Composting with Tea

If you have a compost pile in your garden, always toss your spent tea leaves onto it. Worms adore tea and will help make your compost richer in nitrogen and other nutrients, so it will be good for all your plants, flowers, and vegetables.

## Utilize Those Broken Pots and Cups

Hopelessly broken, cracked, or completely nonfunctional pots and cups can be glued back together and used to hold plant seeds or small garden tools, or to add a bright spot to your greenhouse or garden shed. Teapot lost its lid? That makes it an ideal place to put those small (ugly) plastic pots of herbs or greens to show off the plants in a prettier way.

*Instead of throwing away a broken cup, use it to store small gardening items.*

Oh Mary! soft in feature,
I've been at dear Vauxhall;
No paradise is sweeter,
Not that they Eden call.

Methought when first I
    entered,
Such splendours round me
    shone;
Into a world I entered,
Where rose another sun.

While music never cloying,
As skylarks sweet I hear;
The sounds I'm still enjoying,
They'll always soothe my ear.

— attributed to a "tuneful
    gentleman after a visit to
    Lambeth" in *Amusements
    of Old London*

## MOSAIC TEA LEAF URN

LEVEL OF EXPERTISE:
medium

TOOLS AND MATERIALS:
crockery bowl or jar with
    tight-fitting lid

porcelain shards

various trinkets

coarse-grade sandpaper

mastic (a ceramic adhesive
    sold at hardware and tile
    stores)

large craft stick

paring knife

towel for polishing

You're getting in the habit of saving spent tea leaves to put onto plants, but the amount of tea leaves is getting a little ahead of your plants' nutritional needs. What to do? Create a Mosaic Tea Leaf Urn, a crockery jar, bowl, or similar object with a lid that will help keep the leaves cool and moist, for the times when plants need some "tea fertilizer." This urn is particularly charming when covered with mosaics and shards of broken terra-cotta or porcelain plant pots or — I almost hate to say it — broken teacups and teapots. These catastrophes do happen; if it's a fine teacup, by all means have it repaired. However, if it's not a cup or pot you adore, recycle it into this artful tea urn. Except for the mastic and sandpaper, everything for this project can be found around the house.

If you don't have enough porcelain shards to cover the pot, add other miscellany like buttons, beads, lone earrings who've lost their mates, cracked costume jewelry, porcelain flowers, old holiday ornaments — anything you would normally throw away but could add a dash of color, fun, and whimsy to your tea urn. You could even add some tea tin lids or smashed tins.

1. Wash urn and dry thoroughly. If it has a glazed surface, sand the entire urn and its lid with sandpaper to prepare the pot for gluing on the shards.

2. Arrange the shards and pieces over the urn, trying to match curves to curves. If necessary, break pieces even smaller by covering with a cloth and shattering the pieces with a hammer.

3. Using the craft stick, apply a very thin layer of mastic over the entire surface of the shard to help them adhere to the urn. Always begin with the largest piece. Place the second piece next to the first, and continue until the entire urn is covered. For all exposed gaps or corners, use your trinkets.

**Step 3:** *Apply mastic to the shard before affixing to the urn.*

4. As you apply shards and trinkets to the lid and the top part of the urn, stop frequently to make sure the lid will continue to fit snugly.

5. Allow to dry overnight or at least eight hours.

6. Once dry, apply grout with a craft stick between the shards to help create a smooth surface and protect against any sharp edges. Always wear a dust mask and rubber gloves when applying grout, and follow the directions on the package. Fill every crevice or moisture will creep in and cause rotting.

**Step 6:** *Grout applied between the shards will smooth the surface of the urn.*

7. Using a paring knife, scrape off any excess portions of grout and smooth it out as necessary.

8. Wipe the lid and pot clean with a dry towel and allow the grout to dry until it is hard, about three hours.

9. Polish the dry urn completely with a dry terry towel.

10. Allow to dry another eight hours, and your Mosaic Tea Leaf Urn is ready for its dutiful purpose.

**Step 7:** *Scrape off excess grout with a paring knife.*

# recommended reading

Evans, Charles M., with Roberta Lee Pliner. *The Terrarium Book.* New York: Random House, 1973.

Houser, Preston L. *Invitation to Tea Gardens, Kyoto's Culture Enclosed.* Kyoto: Mitsumura Suiko Shoin Co., Ltd., 1992.

Marshall, Marlene Hurley. *Making Bits & Pieces Mosaics: Creative Projects for Home & Garden.* Pownal: Storey Books, 1998.

Seike, Kiyoshi, Masanobu Kudo, and David H. Engle. *Japanese Touch for Your Garden.* Tokyo: Kodansha International Ltd., 1980.

Tanaka, Sen'o. *The Tea Ceremony.* Tokyo: Kodansha International Ltd., 1973.

Ukers, William H., M.A. *All About Tea, Volume II.* Westport: Hyperion Press, 1994.

Ukers, William H., M.A. *The Romance of Tea, an Outline History of Tea and Tea-Drinking through Sixteen Hundred Years.* New York: Alfred A. Knopf, 1936.

Yoshikawa, Isao. *Japanese Gardening in Small Spaces.* Tokyo: Kodansha International Ltd., 1996.

Yu, Lu. *The Classic of Tea, Origins & Rituals,* translated by Francis Ross Carpenter. Hopewell: The Ecco Press, 1997.

# resources

the following are shops, mail-order companies, and Internet sources for loose-leaf teas and accessories both Western and Oriental. Although there are hundreds more places to buy teas and accessories, this list reflects companies that are known for selling high-quality, loose-leaf teas in the United States. Manufacturers of teas sold in tea bags and available in grocery and natural foods stores are not included in the list because of their wide distribution.

BARNES & WATSON FINE TEAS
1319 Dexter Avenue North, Suite 30
Seattle, WA 98109
(206) 283-6948
Fax (206) 283-0799
*Excellent line of fine teas.*

CAMELLIA TEA COMPANY
P.O. Box 8310
Metairie, LA 70011-8310
(800) 863-3531
Fax (504) 835-3318
*Mail-order catalog with exceptional choices of teas.*

CHADO TEA ROOM
8422½ West Third Street
Los Angeles, CA 90048
(323) 655-2056
*Lovely tearoom and tea shop featuring Mariage Frères teas and other high-end selections and accessories. Mail order is available.*

CHOICE ORGANIC TEAS, GRANUM, INC.
2901 NE Blakely Street
Seattle, WA 98105
(206) 525-0051
Fax (206) 523-9750
*High-quality boxed organic line of teas available at most upscale and health-food stores.*

CORTI BROTHERS
5810 Folsom Boulevard
P.O. Box 191358
Sacramento, CA 95819
(916) 736-3800
Fax (916) 736-3807
*Upscale market and importer of exquisite China teas. Mail order available.*

DEAN & DELUCA
560 Broadway
New York, NY 10012
(212) 431-1691
Fax (212) 334-6183

and
3276 M Street NW, 1299 *and*
1919 Pennsylvania Avenue, NW
Washington, DC
*Upscale markets for loose-leaf and packaged teas of good variety and quality. Mail order available.*

### EAST INDIA TEA AND COFFEE CO., LTD.
1933 Davis Street, Suite 308
San Leandro, CA 94577
(510) 638-1300
Fax (510) 638-0760
*Garden Estate Teas in nicely designed packages.*

### FREED, TELLER & FREED
1326 Polk Street
San Francisco, CA 94109
(415) 673-0922
Fax (415) 673-3436
*Tea to the carriage trade for decades. Good quality. Mail-order catalog.*

### GOLDEN MOON TEA, LTD.
P.O. Box 1646
Woodinville, WA 98072
Fax (206) 881-1765
*Beautifully packaged high-end teas of excellent quality. Mail-order list. Ask about their Limited Reserve Teas.*

### GRACE TEA COMPANY, LTD., NEW YORK
50 West 17th Street
New York, NY 10011
(212) 255-2935
*Winey Keemun and Before the Rain Jasmine are still benchmark teas in a limited but very impressive inventory, elegantly packaged in their signature black tins. Mail-order list.*

### GUY'S TEA/EMPIRE TEA SERVICES
5155 Hartford Avenue
Columbus, IN 47203
(812) 375-1937
Fax (812) 376-7382
Web site: www.guystea.com
e-mail: CeyonTea@JUNO.com
*Excellent selections of teas from Sri Lanka including a 100% Ceylon green.*

### HARNEY & SONS
11 East Main Street Village Green
P.O. Box 638
Salisbury, CT 06068
(888) HARNEY T
Fax (203) 435-5044
Web site: www.harney.com
*Fine teas and accesories from around the world. Stop by for a tasting weekdays at 11 East Brook Street, next to the company office. Mail-order catalog.*

### HIMALAYAN HIGHLAND TEA COMPANY
1702 South Highway 121
Suite 607-189
Lewisville, TX 75067
(800) 580-8585 or (972) 436-1590
Fax (972) 221-6770
*Importers of a variety of teas from Nepal, "Tea Grown on the Roof of the World."*

### HOLY MOUNTAIN TRADING CO.
P.O. Box 457
Fairfax, CA 94978
(650) 757-6149 (Fax/phone)
(888) 832-8008
Web site: www.holymtn.com
*Fine teas and extensive collection of Yixing ware.*

## THE HONORABLE JANE COMPANY
10209 Main Street, P.O. Box 35
Potter Valley, CA 95469
(888) 743-1966
Web site: www.honorablejane.com
e-mail: dearjane@honorablejane.com
*Limited selections of exceptional teas and fine accessories; mail order from their charming catalog.*

## THE HOUSE OF TEA, LTD.
720 South Fourth Street
Philadelphia, PA 19147
(215) 923-8327
*Careful and judicious collection of excellent teas. Visit the shop in Philadelphia or order by mail.*

## IMPERIAL TEA COURT
1411 Powell Street
San Francisco, CA 94133
(415) 788-6080 or (800) 567-5898
Fax (415) 788-6079
Web site: www.imperialtea.com
e-mail: imperial@imperialtea.com
*The first authentic Chinese teahouse in the United States opened in 1995, it has become a popular tourist attraction and a must-see place for China tea lovers. All teas and accessories available by mail order.*

## THE INDOCHINA TEA CO.
P.O. Box 1032
Studio City, CA 91614-0032
(213) 650-8020
Fax (213) 650-8022
*Premium teas from Vietnam.*

## JUNGLESQUE RARE ESTATE COFFEES AND TEAS
Web site: www.junglesque.com
*Exceptional inventory of fine teas from around the world including rare estate teas, Mariage Frères, and other hard-to-find brands.*

## JUSTIN LLOYD PREMIUM TEA CO.
1111 Watson Center Road, Unit A-1
Carson, CA 90745
(310) 834-4400
Fax (310) 834-0300
*Excellent line of fine loose leaf in brilliant red and black "lacquer" tins, and good-quality tea bags.*

## KADO, THE WAY OF FLOWERS
2319 N. 45th Street, Suite 198
Seattle, WA 98103
(206) 409-0675
*Serene and comfortable tearoom in the Seattle Asian Museum offers delicious sweets and exotic teas. Ask for mail-order list.*

## LEAVES PURE LEAVES
1392 Lowrie Avenue
San Francisco, CA 94080
(650) 583-1157
Fax (650) 583-1163
e-mail: Pureteas@leaves.com
*Excellent line of high-quality teas available at Dayton-Hudson and other fine stores.*

## LIBRARY ANTIQUES
70 Spring Street
Williamstown, MA 01267
(800) 294-4798
*Dealer of a variety of fine antiques. Be sure to ask about their gorgeous tea accesories.*

## LINDSAY'S TEAS
380 Swift Avenue, Suite 10
South San Francisco, CA 94080
(650) 871-4845
Fax (650) 952-5446
*Beautifully packaged and carefully blended, the line of teas comes in round colorful canisters.*

## MARIAGE FRÈRES
*(See Chado, Dean & Deluca, The House of Tea, and Junglesque Rare Estate Coffees and Teas.)*

## MARK T. WENDELL, IMPORTER
P.O. Box 1312
West Concord, MA 01742
(978) 369-3709
*If you love Lapsang Souchong, you'll love Hu-Kwa, the jewel in the crown of thirty teas offered by this venerable New England company.*

## THE PEACEFUL DRAGON TEA HOUSE AND CULTURAL CENTER
McMullen Creek Market
8324-509 Pineville-Matthews Rd.
Charlotte, NC 28226
(704) 544-1012
*Enjoy your Chinese teas in Yixing pots, the Japanese teas in ironstone pots, or take a class in Tai Chi before or after tea. Mail order available.*

## RED AND GREEN
191 Potrero Avenue
San Francisco, CA 94103
(415) 626-1375
*Fanciful Yixing teapots and a very credible emerging tea line in sophisticated metal tins.*

## RED CRANE TEAS
2351 Federal Boulevard #405
Denver, CO 80211
(888) 4REDCRANE or (303) 377-3642
e-mail: redcrane@msn.com
*Limited but carefully selected teas that are the highest quality. Available by mail order or via e-mail.*

## THE REPUBLIC OF TEA
8 Digital Drive, Suite 100
Novato, CA 94949
(800) 298-4TEA
Web site: www.sipbysip.com
*New organic line is outstanding and the traditional teas are as delightful as their charming names; good herbals and a nice bottled tea line. Available at fine shops everywhere.*

## ROBERT & JOSEPH, LTD.
6281 Martin Lane
Red Granite, WI 54970-9533
(414) 566-2520 or (414) 566-2275
*A lesser known, albeit dependable, source for quality teas available by mail order.*

## ROYAL GARDENS TEA COMPANY
P.O. Box 1918
Fort Bragg, CA 95437
(707) 961-0263
*Showcases fine teas in beautiful packages. Available in upscale markets, or call for catalog.*

## SARUT, NYC
107 Horatio Street
New York, NY 10014
(212) 691-9453
Web site: www.sarut.com
*Museum-quality gift items that inspire,*

*educate, and entertain. Many Eastern-influenced fragrances, candles, and even tabletop gardens.*

## SERENDIPITEA™

P.O. Box 81
Ridgefield, CT 06877
(888) TEA LIFE or (203) 894-9650
Fax (203) 894-9649
Web site: www.serendipitea.com
*Young, energetic company dedicated to educating your palate and tweaking your senses: exquisite but limited selection of prime teas; clever accessories and emerging beauty care line.*

## SILK ROAD TEAS

P.O. Box 287
Lagunitas, CA 94938
(415) 488-9017
Fax (415) 488-9015
*The Cadillac of teas imported directly from China by owner David Lee Hoffman. Teas are artfully and respectfully packaged, excellent in quality, and worth every penny. Mail-order list.*

## SIMPSON & VAIL INC., QUALITY TEAS & COFFEES SINCE 1929

3 Quarry Road
Brookfield, CT 06804
(800) 282-TEAS or (203) 775-0240
Web site: www.svtea.com
*Mail-order catalog lists a respectable selection of fine teas from around the world. This is the firm that J.P. Morgan trusted to blend his signature tea, still available in addition to more than 120 others.*

## SINOTIQUE

19A Mott Street
New York, NY
(212) 587-2393
*Classes in gung fu; superior selections of teas.*

## SOCIÉTÉ DU THÉ

2516 Lyndale Avenue South
Minneapolis, MN 55405-3319
(888) 871-5148 or (612) 871-5148
Fax (612) 872-1621
Web site: www.la-societe-du-the.com
*Mail-order company and new shop, both carrying exceptional teas from around the world.*

## SPECIALTEAS, INC.

500 Summer Street, Suite 404
Stamford, CT 06901
(888) 365-6983
Fax (203) 975-4566
Web site:www.specialteas.com
*Serious sellers of exceptional teas.*

## STASH TEAS

P.O. Box 910
Portland, OR 97207
(503) 684-4482
Fax (503) 684-4424
(800) 547-1514
Web site: www.stashtea.com
*An impressive collection of fine teas, available in bulk and in several packaged lines: Yamamoto of the Orient (the oldest tea company in Japan), Exotica, and a new line of organic teas. Web site is one of the best on all aspects of tea.*

## TAO OF TEA

3430 SE Belmont
Portland, OR 97214
(503) 736-0119

*Beautiful teahouse designed with warm old woods, copper, and bamboo open daily for sampling extremely rare teas and the classics, all served in the appropriate vessels. Whisked hot and iced matcha are specialties. All-organic, all-vegetarian menu. Yixing pots, accessories, and teas available by mail order.*

## TEAISM, A TEA HOUSE

2009 R Street NW
Washington, DC 20009
(888) 8-TEAISM or (202) 667-3827

*Unusual pan-Asian restaurant devoted to providing education with tea principals from around the world. Carefully selected, high-quality teas from around the world, available by mail order. Restaurant open daily for all meals.*

## TAYLORS OF HARROGATE

Pagoda House, Prospect Road
Harrogate, North Yorkshire
HG2 7NX England
(0423) 889822

*Neiman-Marcus and other upscale shops carry this excellent line of teas, available in both loose-leaf and tea bags.*

## TAZO

P.O. Box 66
Portland, OR 97202
(503) 231-9234
Fax (503) 231-8801

*A fun, fanciful selection of teas from around the world, including refreshing greens made with pure botanicals. Incredible packaging matched by quality teas. Available at most upscale markets.*

## TEA & COMPANY

2207 Fillmore Street
San Francisco, CA 94115
(415) 929-TEAS

*"Starbucks" style tea shop that's hip, hot, and full of fabulous teas. Nice accessories, too. Mail order accepted.*

## TEA COMPANY OF LARKSPUR

100 Larkspur Landing Circle, Suite 104
Larkspur, CA 94939
(415) 925-9936
Fax (415) 925-9833

*Selected high quality teas and accessories. Call for catalog.*

## TEA GARDEN SPRINGS, A SPA FOR NURTURING BODY, MIND AND SOUL

38 Miller Avenue
Mill Valley, CA 94941
(415) 389-7123
Fax (415) 389-7107

*In their lovely atrium, enjoy a cup of Pi Lo Chun before your massage, and a Dragonwell afterward, each served gung fu style. A serene and soothing experience. Teas available for purchase.*

## THE TEA HOUSE, PURVEYORS OF FINE TEAS AND ACCESSORIES

541 Fessler Avenue
Naperville, IL 60565
(630) 961-0877
Fax (630) 961-0817
Web site: www.theteahouse.com

*Excellent line of primarily China teas plus superb selections of flavored teas. Hosts two terrific tours to China yearly, with stops for tea, of course.*

## THE TEA ROOM
7 East Broughton Street
Savannah, GA 31401
(912) 239-9690
*People come for the food, but it's the high-quality teas that surprise. Limited but superb selections from Dragon Pearl Jasmine to Pai Mu Tan Green and other astonishments.*

## TEA TIME
542 Ramona Street
Palo Alto, CA 94301
(650) 328-2877
Web site: www.tea-time.com
*Exceptional selection of fine teas and accessories.*

## THE TEACUP
2207 Queen Avenue North
Seattle, WA 98109
(206) 283-5931
*Very respectable inventory of fine teas and lovely accessories. Mail order.*

## TEAHOUSE KUAN YIN
1911 North 45th Street
Seattle, WA 98103
(206) 632-2055
*and*
Mail Order/Wholesale
1707 North 45th Street
Seattle, WA 98103
(206) 632-2056
Fax (206) 632-8689
*List of very fine teas.*

## TEALUXE
Zero Brattle Street
Harvard Square
Cambridge, MA 02138
(617) 441-0077
Web site: www.tealuxe.com

*If "Cheers" had served tea, this is the place it would be. A fun store right off Harvard Square to enjoy superb teas all day, every day. Teas sold by the gram. An excellent list of teas, brewed by the clock and with great care. Extensive list of other fine teas and accessories for sale or mail order.*

## TEAROOM T
2460 Heather Street
Vancouver, BC
45Z 3H9 Canada
(604) 874-8320
Web site: www.tealeaves.com
*A gathering of the finest estate teas of the world.*

## TEA TALK: A NEWSLETTER ON THE PLEASURES OF TEA
P.O. Box 860
Sausalito, CA 94966
(415) 331-1557
*Diana Rosen's publication on tea. $17.95 for four issues.*

## TEN REN TEA AND GINSENG CO., INC.
75 Mott Street
New York, NY 10013
(212) 349-2286
(800) 292-2049
Fax (212) 349-2180
*and*
135-18 Roosevelt Avenue
Flushing, NY 11354
(718) 461-9305
*Also in Monterey Park and San Francisco, California, and in Chicago, Illinois. Wonderful Formosa teas and other fine loose-leaf teas and accessories.*

## THOMPSON'S FINE TEAS
2062 South Delaware
San Mateo, CA 94403
(800) 830-8835 or (650) 572-9853
Fax (650) 572-9857
Web site: www.fineteas.com
e-mail: Info@fineteas.com
*Limited but very selective inventory of fine teas and accessories, including some from Vietnam.*

## TODD & HOLLAND TEA MERCHANTS
7577 Lake Street
River Forest, IL 60305
(800) 747-8327
Fax (708) 488-1246
Web site: www.todd-holland.com
*Exceptional inventory of fine teas and wonderful information to get you on the road to tea connoisseurship. Store is as elegant and stylish as its teas and accessories. Catalog and newsletter available.*

## UPTON TEA IMPORTS
231 South Street
Hopkinton, MA 01748
(800) 234-TEAS
Web site: www.upton.com
*Tom Eck established this exemplary mail-order company in 1989 and his extensive catalog presently lists about 120 teas from around the world.*

## WATER AND LEAVES
690 Broadway
Redwood City, CA 92063
(800) 699-4753
Fax (415) 952-7907
Web site: www.wayoftea.com
*Elegantly packaged, wonderful China teas, particularly oolongs. Also, Yixing pots. Mail order sales accepted.*

## WINDHAM TEA CLUB
12 Wilson Road
Windham, NH 03087
(800) 565-7527
*Exquisite, carefully selected teas. Windham has a strong commitment to inform with their membership newsletter.*

## WORLD TREASURE TRADING CO.
815 Piner Road
Santa Rosa, CA 95403
(707) 566-7888
Fax (707) 566-7890
*The premier importer of Yixing teaware of both elegant and whimsical designs. All their pots, caddies, and cups are guaranteed to be lead-free and excellent quality. For a store nearest you, call their headquarters.*

# index

Page numbers in *italics* indicate illustration or photos.
Page numbers in **boldface** indicate charts.

# other Storey titles you will enjoy

**The Book of Green Tea,** by Diana Rosen. A comprehensive guide to the history, varieties, and health benefits of this traditional and enjoyable Asian beverage. Includes recipes for food and beauty and health care products. 160 pages. Paperback. ISBN 1-58017-090-0.

**Country Tea Parties,** by Maggie Stuckey. Organized by month, this book offers interesting, creative ideas for 12 special tea parties. Beautiful four-color illustrations by Carolyn Bucha highlight the menus and recipes. 64 pages. Hardcover. ISBN 0-88266-935-4.

**Herbal Tea Gardens: 23 Plans for Your Enjoyment and Well-Being,** by Marietta Marshall Marcin. This handy reference book contains valuable information on growing a garden for herbal teas. Included are nearly 100 plant profiles, gardening information, harvesting and storage tips, brewing instructions, and 23 garden plans customized to your special health and landscape needs. 192 pages. Paperback. ISBN 1-58017-106-0.

**Keeping Entertaining Simple,** by Martha Storey. This fun-to-read tips book offers hundreds of ideas for low-fuss, low-anxiety entertaining with friends, for the holidays, and for business purposes. 160 pages. Paperback. ISBN 1-58017-056-0.

**Tea with Friends,** by Elizabeth Knight. A year's worth of occasions to bring friends together around a pot of tea. Each party contains suggested menus and activities, and includes elegant watercolor paintings by noted Caspari artist Carolyn Bucha. 64 pages. Hardcover. ISBN 1-58017-050-1.

*These books and other Storey books are available at your bookstore, farm store, garden center, or directly from Storey Publishing, Schoolhouse Road, Pownal, Vermont 05261, or by calling 1-800-441-5700. Or visit our Web site at www.storey.com.*